the **CYCLE TOUR**

MIKE WILLS

with a foreword by PHIL LIGGETT

DOUBLE STOREY
a juta company

Cape Argus
Pick n Pay
CYCLE TOUR
ROTARY · PPA

the CYCLE TOUR

First published 2008
Double Storey Books
a division of Juta & Co. Ltd.
Mercury Crescent, Wetton, 7780
Cape Town, South Africa

www.doublestorey.com

ISBN: 978-1-770-13065-4
1 2 3 4 5 6 7 8 9 10

PUBLISHER **Colleen Hendriksz**
PROJECT MANAGER **Sarah O'Neill**
DESIGNER **Pete Bosman**
EDITOR **Jennifer Stern**
PRINTED AND BOUND BY **Craft Print International Ltd, Singapore**

contents

ABOVE **Phil Liggett—The voice of cycling. The TV commentator, famous for his coverage of the Tour de France, has been involved with the Cycle Tour for 17 years.**

FOREWORD

by Phil Liggett

When 525 riders set off to ride around the Cape Peninsula in 1978 by way of a protest over the lack of facilities for cyclists on Cape roads, they could never have foreseen that 30 years later 'their' event would have blossomed into the biggest of its kind anywhere in the world. In 2008, another 35,000 riders will enjoy one of the most beautiful routes a cyclist could hope to encounter and Cape Town, perhaps mindful of the protests of 1978, will again open its arms to welcome cyclists of every shape and size from around the globe.

ABOVE Phil Liggett (centre) in Cape Town with former Tour de France champions Jan Ullrich (left) and Greg LeMond (right).

To me, Cape Town and 'the Argus', with apologies to gracious sponsor, Pick n Pay, are synonymous and, since seeing my first event in 1990, I've never missed one. It is infectious and if you have not 'done the Argus', then you have missed out on a special slice of your life.

Of course, it is now a major money spinner for Cape Town, charities benefit enormously and professional riders practise their sport to the full. In short, there are no losers on this most wonderful of occasions in the March of every year.

During the 30 years of the Cycle Tour, cycling as both a sport and a pastime has become more popular everywhere, from Australia to Andorra and from Cape Town to Canada. But it is in South Africa, particularly, that this pastime has grown out of all proportion. In 2007, a Cycle Tour winner, Robbie Hunter became the first South African rider to win a stage in the Tour de France. Now that is progress!

As long as I'm able, I will never miss the Cape Argus Pick n Pay Cycle Tour as, to me, as it is for thousands of others, it's the greatest one-day event in the world.

This beautiful book from Mike Wills will take you through a dream, which started in 1978 and has come true in every way.

PHIL LIGGETT
TV COMMENTATOR
HERTFORD, UK 2007

ABOVE **Cyclists on Klein Chappies taking in the spectacular sight of Long Beach with Kommetjie in the distance.**

INTRODUCTION

So many magical moments.

The fresh, tense optimism of the mass start on a golden autumn dawn under the watchful eye of the defining mountain.

The high-speed charge along the twisting False Bay shore.

Misty Cliffs where, without fail, the wind seems to die, and riders are almost able to touch the intensely azure sea and the sharp white sand.

Looking back in wonder from Klein Chappies over the majestic sweep of Long Beach towards the Kommetjie Lighthouse.

The crest of Chapman's Peak and the panorama of Hout Bay.

And, for everyone, there's the top of the infamous Suikerbossie, when you can peer down on postcard Llandudno with the tired, gloating elation that, in Sir Edmund Hillary's words after conquering Everest, you have 'knocked the bugger off'.

The Cape Argus Pick n Pay Cycle Tour takes place in cycling heaven—a 109 km circuit from the old heart of Cape Town down the eastern side of the Table Mountain chain to the Cape Point gate of the Table Mountain National Park, and then back up the Atlantic coastline—sometimes on torturous climbs hewn out of the cliff face—to the finish on Green Point Common, the city's historic place of recreation. Two-thirds of the race takes place in a designated nature reserve and world heritage site.

The route, with a couple of minor adjustments, remains remarkably faithful to the one set up by the Tour's founders who began it all in 1978 as part of their campaign for cycle paths in Cape Town. They were challenged by the city authorities to demonstrate that there was support for the sport they loved and, after a successful ride-in protest, they decided to hold a race right round the scenic peninsula. The *Argus* newspaper gave the venture both publicity and its name, and 525 cyclists started that very first Argus Cycle Tour, battling their way through traffic on un-cleared roads.

Ironically, 30 years later, the campaign for cycle paths has borne little or no fruit in Cape Town but 'the Argus', as it became universally known, has mushroomed into one of the world's great participatory sporting events with local, individual entries capped at 35,000. Many more knock on the door each year but the city's narrow roads can't safely cope with everyone who wants to take part. It's grown into the biggest timed cycle race on the planet, and provides an estimated annual injection of R350 m into the Cape economy.

The Tour is a reasonably competitive challenge for the pros, often acting as the final stage of the *Giro del Capo*, and attracting members of the sport's global elite like Alexandre Vinokourov and Robbie Hunter, but its iconic status on the international cycling calendar is primarily because of its appeal for amateur riders who, whether they deliver a serious sub-three hour time or struggle through in more than six hours, can, for this one day, feel part of the kind of special sporting experience in such a memorable environment that is usually reserved only for the top echelon.

The first 30 years of the Tour saw over 150,000 different people completing the race in times somewhere between the all-comers' record of 2:16:40 and the official cut-off of seven hours. Thousands more enter but don't make the start line while many fall out en route, a sharp reminder that, for all its accessibility and broad appeal, the Cycle Tour remains a test that can easily be underestimated. It also carries clear and present dangers for anyone in a fast-moving pack or speeding downhill. And, as heavenly as the route is, it can become hellish in the hands of the Cape weather gods. Although March is traditionally a benign time of year on the southern tip of Africa, wind, rain, cold and heat have all wreaked havoc at various times.

1987 is remembered as The Year of the Storm, when visibility, at times, was reduced to a few metres by what was described as 'an icy monsoon'. In startling contrast, the 2002 De-Tour (one of four years the race was diverted away from Chapman's Peak because the road was being re-built) saw temperatures above 40° on the draining 7 km climb up Ou Kaapse Weg, and the course was closed early by the concerned medical team.

The classic Cape Doctor, a wind from the south-east, plays a varying part every year—almost always cruelly hitting the late-starting backmarkers far harder than the much fitter front-runners who ride in the gentler, early morning airs—but 2005 produced brutish headwinds of up to 60 km/h that blew several competitors off their bikes, and made even the usually relaxed freeway ride down the Blue Route a tiring slog.

But none of the notorious years has stunted the relentless growth in the popularity of the Tour (entries almost doubled following the freezing horrors of 1987), and the fact that the tough times stand out in memory indicates that the Argus has generally been ridden in reasonable conditions.

OPPOSITE **The Cycle Tour threading its way past Glencairn Station on False Bay between Fish Hoek & Simon's Town.**

As the event has grown, so has its demands. Since 1982 the Rotary Club has been involved alongside the Pedal Power Association as organisers and beneficiaries. Their nominated charities have received millions of rands and, in return, Rotary has marshalled thousands of selfless volunteers who each year provide the essential infrastructure for such a massive event, backing up a full-time Cycle Tour staff of eight.

Retail giant Pick n Pay came on board in 1991 with a major sponsorship that enabled the Tour to continue to meet the needs of the ever-growing number of cyclists, as well as the community projects the event funds.

And the city authorities, once so sceptical of cycling's popularity, now understand its value for Cape Town. Unlike those first hardy competitors, Tour entrants now travel along 109 km of clear roads, including many major freeways—a logistical exercise that requires the co-ordination of hundreds of police officers and the forbearance of hundreds of thousands of city residents as their usual routes are closed, in some instances for an entire Sunday.

Most of those inconvenienced respond by setting up camp on their pavements and cheering the Tour past their front doors. Muizenberg, St James, Kalk Bay, Fish Hoek, Simon's Town, Scarborough, Ocean View, Noordhoek, Hout Bay and, above all, Suikerbossie have become community carnival points from early morning almost until the sweeper vans come through. There is an overwhelming sense of goodwill and good humour that the Cycle Tour brings onto the streets of the Cape Peninsula every year.

ABOVE **Suikerbossie. The Cycle Tour's signature hill with the ever-present carnival of supporters.**
OPPOSITE **The bike park at Green Point Stadium needed to be able to accommodate 25,000 bicycles.**

In South Africa, cycling is now a radically different sport compared to 1978. Then it had its dedicated devotees, and some exceptionally talented cyclists, but it was viewed by many as little more than a childish pastime for 'the very poor, the weirdos and the racers,' according to co-founder John Stegmann. The 1980s changed all that with the fitness fad spreading, gyms proliferating with banks of exercise bikes, and the development of reasonably cheap and robust mountain bikes creating an entirely new entry point for the sport. The end of apartheid sporting isolation opened windows of opportunity for the best in the world to enter, and for the local elite to openly test themselves in the international arena. The final piece in the jigsaw was the intensive coverage given by Supersport to the Tour de France, literally bringing home to South Africans the extraordinary drama and phenomenal athleticism of cycling at its very best. Throughout the 1980s word increasingly spread that the Argus was a superb experience for everyone, not just fanatical cyclists, and by 1990 close to 15,000 people were entering, and Supersport had been broadcasting extensive highlights for three years.

By this point the Cycle Tour had become far more than a sporting event—it was a massive commercial and logistical operation that had moved way beyond the original vision of the founders. As growth continued through the 1990s and into the new millennium, those entrusted with the Tour's fate have had to maintain a series of difficult balances—between the event and the environment, the business and the bikes, between the pros and the amateurs and, within the unpaid ranks, between the fun riders and the fanatics. That they have, by and large, met those challenges successfully is clear from the record demands, domestically and internationally, for the 31st edition. And the evidence can also be found in the extraordinary array of cyclists on the start line—from the edgy racers at 06h15 through to the costumed jokers at 10h30.

Inevitably, difficult tasks remain for the organisers. In spite of intense efforts to spread its appeal, including substantial development squads and the highly publicised participation of several ANC cabinet members, the Cycle Tour continues to attract an overwhelmingly white field. Cycling as a cheap, mass means of transport has not caught on to any great degree in South Africa, especially when contrasted with the millions of pedallers you'll find in a Beijing peak hour. Security undoubtedly has much to do with it, as cyclists feel vulnerable to crime, and also to bad drivers. While, on race day, the clear roads of the Cape Argus Pick n Pay Cycle Tour provide probably the longest and safest stretch of cycling security that you would find anywhere in the world, on every other day of the year the roads of Cape Town and all major urban areas of the country are a dangerous lottery for bike riders. The Pedal Power Association has been campaigning hard to rectify this problem, but it's proving an uphill task greater than tackling Suikerbossie after 95 hot, windswept kilometres.

But there's no doubt the Cycle Tour enters its fourth decade in exceptionally good health. The great majority of entrants ride more than once. There are so many reasons to keep coming back for one more crack at a better time or for one more chance to savour some of the world's most spectacular scenery in the best possible way—by earning the right to be there through the power of your legs and lungs.

Every year there are just so many magical moments on the Cape Argus Pick n Pay Cycle Tour.

TOP **Defence Minister Mosuioa Lekota has completed five Cycle Tours.**
ABOVE **The Cycle Tour 1970's style— helmets only became compulsory in 1990.**
OPPOSITE **Lion's Head in the background as riders face their first challenge, the climb out of the city up Eastern Boulevard.**

THE ROUTE

The 109 km of the Cycle Tour route include an extraordinary range of roads and surfaces from smooth, wide open freeways to tight, bumpy suburban streets.

Riders are basically travelling due south for the first half of the race, often into the teeth of the prevailing south-easter, but from the top of Smitswinkel it's primarily a northerly journey home.

The early climbs up Eastern Boulevard, past the University of Cape Town and over Wynberg Hill are often underestimated because legs are fresh but the latter point is the highest reached on the Tour apart from Chapman's Peak.

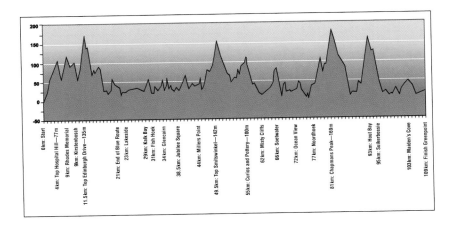

1   From the city centre behind Table Mountain in the distance the Cycle Tour heads south to False Bay and Fish Hoek beach (centre).

2   From False Bay the route runs up over Smitswinkel and across the back of the Cape Point peninsular to the Atlantic Ocean at Misty Cliffs then on to Chapman's Peak (top centre).

3   From Chapman's Peak the Cycle Tour moves through Hout Bay, up over Suikerbossie (left centre) and down along the coastline.

4   From Camps Bay (far right) the route winds above the Clifton beaches and through Bantry Bay and Sea Point (lower centre) before finishing at Green Point Stadium.

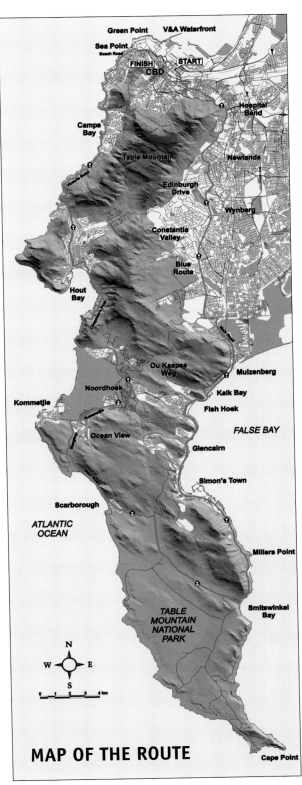

MAP OF THE ROUTE

The start

The official start-line of the Cycle Tour is on Hertzog Boulevard on the east side of the city centre of Cape Town, but the start area colonises a square kilometre towards Heerengracht to allow for holding pens for 57 different seeded groups, repair shops, portaloos, first aid posts, a control centre, TV cameras, tog bag deposits, timing zones and thousands of spectators. At 06h15 the elite group race off into the dawn light. They are followed for more than four hours, like clockwork, by a group starting every five minutes alternating between both sides of the wide boulevard—each of them sent on their way with the famous 'Hoop-La' from the long-serving official starter Paul de Groot. Riders pass right underneath the massive Civic Centre building, and enjoy only 0.5 km of flat road before hitting the first uphill challenge.

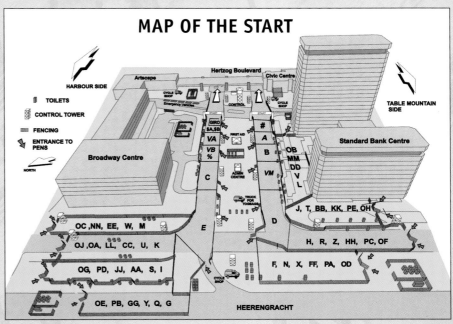

MAP OF THE START

HARBOUR SIDE

TOILETS

CONTROL TOWER

FENCING

ENTRANCE TO PENS

NORTH

Artscape

Hertzog Boulevard

Civic Centre

TABLE MOUNTAIN SIDE

CYCLE SHOP

Emergency Vehicles

CONTROL

CYCLE SHOP

GIRO $A, $B

VA

VB %

C

FIRST AID

#

A

B

VM

Standard Bank Centre

OB MM DD V L

Broadway Centre

ADMIN CENTRE

TRUCK FOR TOGBAGS

J, T, BB, KK, PE, OH

OC ,NN, EE, W, M

OJ ,OA, LL, CC, U, K

OG, PD, JJ, AA, S, I

E

D

H, R, Z, HH, PC, OF

F, N, X, FF, PA, OD

CYCLE SHOP

OE, PB, GG, Y, Q, G

HEERENGRACHT

RIGHT The map of the start zone in central Cape Town shows the holding pens for the 57 different seeded groups necessary for 35,000 riders.

City to Surf

The 3 km climb out of the city, past District Six and up Eastern Boulevard is an instant wake-up call for any under-prepared rider, especially in a stiff south-easter. The classic frontal view of Table Mountain is on the right but nervous cyclists are more likely to be checking the median strip palm trees as an early indicator of the strength of the wind—if the fronds are flapping hard then its going to be a tough day in the saddle.

From the crest of Eastern Boulevard there is a tempting, high-speed, 1 km sweep down through Hospital Bend. It's the first descent of the Tour and, being so close to the start, groups are still tightly bunched. The result is often catastrophic, with as many as 50 bikes being taken down on one occasion. Thankfully Groote Schuur Hospital, scene of the world's first-ever heart transplant in 1967, is only metres away for casualties.

The Tour bends right along the M3, and through a glorious mountain-backed sequence of the Rhodes Estate, the University of Cape Town, and Newlands Forest before swinging down Paradise Road to the foot of Edinburgh Drive. The 2 km climb up Wynberg Hill is usually packed with spectators—and with riders—as the field is yet to really spread out.

The slog up the hill is instantly rewarded with the chance to fly down the freeway and onto the Blue Route—10 km of high-speed pack riding that ends with a sharp left into Steenberg Road at Westlake Golf Course, and an almost immediate right onto Main Road to head for Muizenberg.

ABOVE **Heading out of the city up Eastern Boulevard.**
RIGHT **Pack-riding along the Blue Route freeway.**

False Bay

The famous breakers of Muizenberg Beach greet the cyclists 25 km into the course as they begin to tackle the scenic, twisting False Bay coast road, which only has the railway line between it and the sea. The views across the bay to Hangklip are spectacular, but experienced riders will keep their eyes firmly on the treacherous surface that includes plenty of manhole covers. The colourful beach changing sheds of St James mean a quarter of the route has been completed and, after 28 km, the bars and coffee shops of the picturesque fishing village of Kalk Bay are irresistible for the more leisurely cycle tourists at the back of the field.

Clovelly, Fish Hoek, Sunny Cove and Glencairn, all with their supportive residents out on the street, flash by, and one-third of the Tour is done when the riders reach the heart of historic Simon's Town and the always vibrant refreshment station on Jubilee Square.

Heading out of Simon's Town past the Naval Dockyard, Boulder's Beach and the golf course, there are a couple of beguiling downhill stretches—including one that ends at the delightfully-named Rumbly Bay—before what is, for many, the toughest section of the route—the 5 km haul to the top of Smitswinkel.

**Historic Simon's Town, home of the South African
Navy, is always a major tour landmark.**

Smits and the Outback

The climb to Smits is not particularly demanding on a still day but such days are rare in this part of the world, and the south-easter usually pumps into the faces of riders from the clearly visible Cape Point. Baboons abound on this stretch as they brazenly scavenge for scraps and detritus being shed by slow-moving cyclists. The steep part of the ascent begins at Partridge Point, and the extraordinary views way down to the isolated Smitswinkel beach cottages, across the bay and out to sea, are no compensation for the false hopes that are dashed with each corner of the climb before the huge cedar tree that marks the summit is finally sighted, and then reached, just short of the entrance to the Cape Point section of the Table Mountain National Park.

The 8 km stretch of largely shaded, undulated riding that follows Smits offers a welcome relief, but is somewhat soulless. Aside from the prospect of spying ostriches at the Cape Point Ostrich Farm, and the encouraging news that you have passed the half-way mark at Klaasjagersberg, this is an inland, featureless and empty stretch, often referred to as 'The Outback', with no crowds, and a long way still to go.

Camel Rock to Chappies

Relief from the Outback comes at the 58 km mark with the left turn to Scarborough, which is marked by a massive carved elephant outside the Sculpture Garden. The downhill from the corner towards the Atlantic Ocean is the first of significance since Wynberg Hill and, as a result, is often tackled with too much enthusiasm. The descent is deceptively tricky, and claims many casualties. The holiday town of Scarborough is completely isolated by the road closures for the Cycle Tour, but the residents happily camp on the kerb and cheer everyone past Camel Rock, their famous landmark.

Misty Cliffs is next, and usually provides one of the most exhilarating sections of the Tour—a couple of kilometres of slight downhill as close to the ocean as it's possible to be without getting sand on your tyres. For slower riders it's a revitalising experience to smell the salt spray and enjoy the view out beyond the crayfish factory on the point before working hard again up the hill to Soetwater, where the race turns briefly inland again onto Slangkop Road.

At the 67 km mark the full extent of the challenges that lie ahead become all too real, as both Chapman's Peak and Suikerbossie come clearly into distant view.

The township of Ocean View always provides noisy support shortly thereafter as does the community of Masiphumelele before reaching the left turn onto Ou Kaapse Weg at Sun Valley. After a further 1 km, with two-thirds of the race done, the Tour turns left again and heads for Noordhoek, which offers a shady respite before Chappies and the first part of the climb, which is only 1.5 km. Novice riders are often conned into thinking they have cracked the infamous peak at this point, but this is only Klein (Little) Chappies, with its breathtaking views south along Long Beach to the Kommetjie Lighthouse (which was a prominent landmark on the first 22 tours before the town was cut from the route).

The 2 km haul up Chappies proper is the signature section of the Tour. A long, snaking line of cyclists appears to be clinging to the side of the precipitous mountainside with huge, ominous catch-fences above to, hopefully, trap any falling rocks. The engineering involved in the toll road with its tunnels and natural rock overhangs is a wonder to behold, but it is rarely appreciated by the straining cyclists.

The top of Chapman's Peak, and the view of the awesome Sentinel above the fishing village of Hout Bay, is one of the great rewards for the recreational riders but the elite racers will barely notice as they stretch their racing legs on the winding, 5 km descent to the toll gates and the iconic statue of a leopard on a rock.

The Bay and the Bossie

Hout Bay is the calm between two storms, with Chappies conquered but Suikerbossie still lying in wait. The three-quarter mark is reached in the town which provides a warm welcome, and cooling sprays from garden hoses for the passing parade through Main Road, Princess Street and then north along Victoria Street from a traffic circle that has the extraordinary folly of Liechtenstein Castle looming over it.

After 91km, the final serious test begins. The front runners won't be troubled by the constant 2km climb up Suikerbossie but everyone else will be, and the massage stations are busy right through the day as cramp takes a hold on tired legs. Support is phenomenal for the entire length of the climb throughout the day, as the crowd settles in with their traditional skottel braais and blaring music, and often push wilting riders up the hill. At the summit, many cyclists punch the air in triumph and then relish the sight of exclusive Llandudno glistening far below.

OPPOSITE Victoria Road heading up through the heart of Hout Bay
with the torturous climb to Suikerbossie in the distance.
ABOVE The crowded summit of Suikerbossie.

Cruising home

The Tour has a gentle and undemanding final 15 km. The long downhill from Suikerbossie offers sights of the Atlantic Seaboard in its full glory—the Twelve Apostles, Camps Bay, Signal Hill and Robben Island are all in view. The route flattens out at the bright, white Twelve Apostles Hotel and then goes through Bakoven and past the beach-goers and cappuccino drinkers of bustling Camps Bay, where the Bay Hotel hides the distinctive Rotunda building that marked the finish line of the first 12 Cycle Tours. A short uphill leads to Maiden's Cove, where the next 10 tours ended and the carnival used to be held. But now the Tour races on above the famous beaches of Clifton and through the streets of Bantry Bay, two of the country's most expensive residential areas. Then a sharp left and right turn in quick succession take the riders onto the Sea Point sea-front and past its pines, palms and towering apartments.

The finish

After 109 km of exhausting, exhilarating riding, the Tour ends on Western Boulevard in Green Point alongside the old stadium. The competitors for line honours hustle at a desperate full tilt through the narrow channel, and others will deliver a final sprint if a personal best time is still a possibility, but for most it's done at a gentle, thankful pedalling pace with a sense of great relief and achievement.

The massive logistical expanse of the start is replicated at the finish with timing systems, medal distribution, drinks and first aid all available immediately, and a giant bike park and carnival area provided for the celebrating cyclists and their supporters.

OPPOSITE The old Green Point
Stadium, now demolished, provided
the bike park at the finish from
1999 to 2006.
ABOVE Some walk, some ride but all
are happy to see the finish line.
RIGHT Teams of masseurs bring
welcome relief to tired bodies
and cramping legs.

The De-Tour

From 2000–2003 the closure of Chapman's Peak forced the organisers to establish a four year
De-Tour which bypassed Hout Bay and the Atlantic Seaboard completely.

The route was the same as the one currently used until Sun Valley where, instead of turning
left towards Noordhoek and Chappies, riders continued on Ou Kaapse Weg and up the notorious,
exposed, 7 km climb to Silvermine. The subsequent descent to Tokai was the most dangerous
ever included in the Tour, and organisers took special precautions with stacked hay bales at
the vicious hairpin bend towards the bottom. Riders then did the first quarter of the race in
reverse and discovered that the Blue Route wasn't as flat inbound as it appeared on the outward
leg. Wynberg Hill was also more of a challenge from the south on tired legs than it was from
the north on fresh ones. Paradise Road and Hospital Bend presented further demands before a
comfortable sweep down Eastern Boulevard and through the city centre to Green Point, which
was reached from the opposite direction to the current finish.

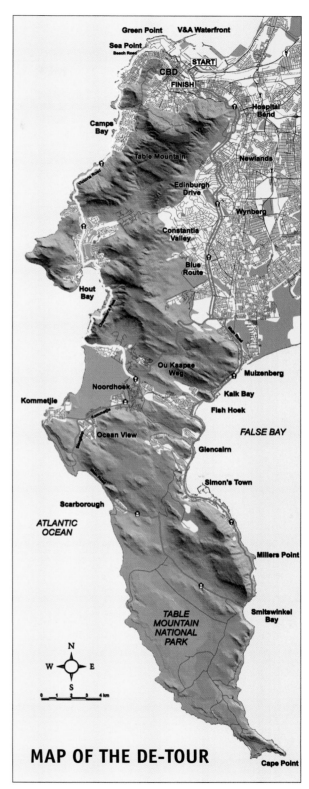

MAP OF THE DE-TOUR

ABOVE **The climb up Hospital Bend provided the last challenge of the De-Tour route.**

OPPOSITE **The De-Tour in–out effect; the leading pack hurtle towards the finish as later starters head up towards the University of Cape Town with 105 km still to go.**

1 >>

2 >>

The drama

The Cycle Tour is never without drama. The expert medical teams are constantly in action, attending to everything from minor scrapes to, on several occasions, heart attacks.

Cape Argus photographer Jim McLagan captured this spectacular, high-speed pile-up on Hospital Bend in 2007—amazingly there were no serious injuries.

5 >>

3 >>

4 >>

ABOVE **The popular Robbie McIntosh after his Cycle Tour win in 1983.
He claimed the title again in 1991.**

THE HISTORY

The Cape Argus Pick n Pay Cycle Tour has been described as the most successful failure in sporting history. The race began as merely one part of a campaign for the establishment of a network of safe cycling paths around Table Mountain. Those paths remain un-built, and Cape Town's crowded roads are still a dangerous place for everyday cyclists. So, in that sense, the Tour has failed, but in every other way it has been a success far beyond the dreams of its founders.

Bill Mylrea and John Stegmann are the two, almost accidental, visionaries who in 1977 conceived the notion of a testing, long, cycling event through the Cape's spectacular scenery. Mylrea was a building contractor who also had an outlet selling bikes and mopeds; his friend Stegmann was an architect, and they had both re-discovered their youthful enthusiasm for cycling in their 30s. Appropriately, the idea cropped up on one of their regular rides together as they kicked around suggestions for making their sport more popular and thereby, they hoped, increasing demand for the kind of protected cycling routes commonly found in Europe.

Both men knew they wanted a real examination of cycling skills and fitness that would generate a sense of achievement for all who finished. Mylrea was keen to have a two-day event that took in parts of the Boland mountain ranges as well but they settled for Stegmann's original notion of 'the Castle to the Lighthouse and back'. Neither of them had ridden the route—or anything remotely as long as it—in their lives and got 'quite a surprise' when they realised just how testing their chosen challenge would prove to be.

ABOVE John Stegmann (top) and Bill Mylrea in 2007, 30 years after the two close friends and passionate cyclists inspired the first Cycle Tour.
LEFT Riders without helmets battle Chapman's Peak and the traffic during an early Tour.

Stegmann and Mylrea were both active members of the newly-formed Western Province Pedal Power Association, which became the organising body for what was initially to be called the Peninsula Marathon, and was scheduled for September 1978 over 140 km.

Intense negotiations were required with various sets of officials to gain permission for the use of the route by a group of riders who were perceived as more of a traffic nuisance than groundbreaking athletes. The authorities made a key concession when they allowed cyclists early morning access to the previously forbidden Blue Route freeway, but they would not permit a return journey into the city centre at a busier time so the finish had to be at Camps Bay, where it remained until 2000.

The most significant change from the original blueprint came when the Tour was refused entrance to the Cape Point Nature Reserve (now part of the Table Mountain National Park) on the grounds of likely environmental damage. The park's guardians were probably not justified in their concerns about that very first Tour but they have been vindicated since, as it's scarcely conceivable that 35,000 cyclists, and the support facilities that go with them, would leave the environs in pristine condition—diligent as the annual clean-up operation is.

The Nature Conservation ban deprived riders of the special thrill of reaching the legendary Cape Point but, in slicing 35 km off the planned route, they may have done the Cycle Tour a long-term favour by reducing the distance to a more manageable one for the legions of four-hour-plus riders who make up the majority of the entrants and—as much as the extraordinary landscape—give the Tour its unique character.

ABOVE The baboons have been ever-present spectators throughout the Tour's history.
OPPOSITE TOP The start of the first Cycle Tour with 525 entrants.
OPPOSITE BELOW Lawrence Whittaker (Right) winner of the inaugural Cycle Tour with runner-up Wimpie van der Merwe, who would, 15 years later, set a course record on a recumbent bike that still stands.

This mass appeal was not an accident. From the very first Tour, it was an inclusive event that anyone could ride without qualification. Plenty of warnings were issued about the need for training, and that the cut-off time of eight-and-a-half hours would be enforced. However, everyone who had paid their entry fee was entitled to be on the start line, and from the outset there were categories of achievement and benchmarks for every standard. There was a risk that this might alienate elite riders or in some way reduce the status of the event but, in fact, the reverse happened and its overwhelming broad popularity immediately made it a must-win race for any South African professional's career record, even if it is far from the most technically demanding ride on the calendar.

The Peninsula Marathon never happened. The Western Province Pedal Power Association understood the need for media backing, and convinced an initially reluctant *Cape Argus* newspaper to back the infant event by granting it naming rights. So it was on 29 August 1978 that entries opened for the Argus Cycle Tour, and race day was set for Saturday 26 October.

The following year it shifted forward to its familiar autumn timeslot, but it was only in 1990 that the event, having got too big for a commercial Saturday, was moved to a more sedate Sunday in the face of religious objections.

1978

525 entrants
446 finishers
Men's Winner: Lawrence Whittaker 3:02:25
Women's Winner: Janice Theis 4:35:00

This seemingly humble start already represented Africa's biggest cycle race.

The registered racers were not permitted to ride with the 'recreationals', as they were called, but a compromise was reached that allowed both groups to take part in the same event by starting at different times. This meant that each rider needed an individual time to determine the winners. This would prove to be the signature of the event, and separate it from every ride of equivalent size anywhere in the world.

Cannon fire from the Castle was meant to signal the two different starts, but the first attempt failed to produce any explosion, and the second reportedly destroyed the makeshift cannon!

The recreationals went off first, followed 10 minutes later by the contenders for top honours who swept past the main body of the field before they reached UCT. Each entrant carried a piece of paper that had to be stamped at the start, Muizenberg, the Cape Point gate, Kommetjie and the finish.

Throughout the race, riders had to contend with traffic on un-cleared roads and nagging crosswinds. Western Province road racing champion Lawrence Whittaker etched his name in Argus history after a shoulder-to-shoulder dice with Springbok Wimpie van der Merwe along Main Road, Camps Bay to the finish line opposite the old Rotunda Hotel (now the Bay Hotel). Whittaker recalls winning by 'about half a wheel' thus ensuring himself a lifelong calling card as 'the man who won the first Argus'. His female counterpart, Janice Theis, struggled through in what now seems a pedestrian 4:35, but she would return the following year with far better preparation to slash almost an hour off her winning time.

> John Stegmann rode the first tandem home accompanied by his 10-year-old son Richard, a feat they were to repeat for the next two years. Stegmann says they walked up most of the hills.

> At the back of the pack, the last three riders to cross the line had stopped off at the Kommetjie Hotel for a reviving beer and some lunch before completing their exhausting journey.

ABOVE **Hans Degenaar's 1979 win was overshadowed by events in the, then, Rhodesia.**
ABOVE RIGHT **The 1980 Tour marked the start of the revitalised Cape Town Festival.**

1979

999 entrants
760 finishers
Men's Winner: Hans Degenaar 2:52:38
Women's Winner: Janice Theis 3:36:46

The second Tour was held less than six months later to take advantage of better March weather, and to align it with other city and Argus-sponsored events. Already the Cycle Tour was on an exponential growth curve with the number of entrants virtually doubling to one short of a thousand. The long-term future of the event also looked bright, as more than 100 of the riders were under the age of 15. A trio of Stellenbosch riders dominated a much faster men's race with Springbok Hans Degenaar taking the honours from Pierre Smit and the previous year's runner-up, Wimpie van der Merwe. Lawrence Whittaker was fourth. Degenaar and Smit were later to link up to win the tandem category in 1987, and van der Merwe would be first man home in 1993 on a recumbent bike. Janice Theis recorded her massively improved winning time in spite of what she described as 'a lot of mechanical trouble'.

1980

1,398 entrants
1,119 finishers
Men's winner: Hennie Wentzel 3:02:18
Women's winner: Sharon Broekhuyzen 3:51:00

The Cycle Tour was the opening event for the revived Cape Town Festival. With over a thousand riders completing the race, Springbok Hennie 'Wiele' Wentzel was first home in a surprisingly slow time given that race conditions were described as 'fine and mild'. But there was nothing mild about the finish—one of the most hectic in race history. Stellenbosch rider Rassie Smit was first home, but was disqualified under heavy protest for slip-streaming his team vehicle. As the leading pack of six sprinters were confronted with a bus that had stopped to drop off passengers in Camps Bay, inaugural winner Lawrence Whittaker opted for the gap on the right between the bus and a traffic policeman, and finished second to Wentzel, who chose to dart left alongside the pavement and through the startled alighting bus passengers.

ABOVE **Ertjies Bezuidenhout led a record-breaking pack to win in 1981.**
BELOW **UCT student Mark Pinder was the surprise champion in 1982.**

1981

1,669 entrants
1,372 finishers
Men's winner: Ertjies Bezuidenhout 2:47:42
Women's winner: Ann Wood 3:40:01

To avoid congestion at the bottom of Eastern Boulevard, the start was moved back from the Castle to its current space on Hertzog Boulevard beside the stark concrete tower block of the Civic Centre. Another record-breaking field headed off into a fog that was so thick around parts of False Bay that the riders couldn't even see the water. Yet another Springbok cyclist, Ertjies Bezuidenhout, won the event in record time, finishing ahead of Gerrie Genis with the luckless Wimpie van der Merwe in third place. The first 12 riders all finished inside the old mark.

1982

1,698 entrants
1,347 finishers
Men's winner: Mark Pinder 3:01:25
Women's winner: Martina le Roux 3:34:54

A day of howling wind produced the most remarkable upset in the history of the Cycle Tour. Although Ertjies Bezuidenhout was once again first across the line he had to concede the fastest time to an unseeded rider (officially described as 'unregistered'). University of Cape Town student, Mark Pinder, finished just behind the leading bunch but had started five minutes

ABOVE 2,300 entrants at the start in 1983 when (above right) William Smith and Francois du Toit rode their tandem to line honours.

later so, on corrected time, was declared the winner. Pinder was the last men's winner to take more than three hours. The south-easter was so strong that the start banner couldn't be raised, a starting pole blew onto a competitor, and even a seasoned pro like Bezuidenhout took 15 minutes longer to complete the course than the previous year (not helped by missing the turn to Chapman's Peak and briefly heading up Ou Kaapse Weg!). There was also serious traffic chaos in Simon's Town where angry motorists were confronted by road works, and roads full of bikes. All of which made Martina le Roux's record-breaking time for a female rider an impressive achievement.

The Rotary Club of Claremont began its hugely successful partnership with the Western Province Pedal Power Association, who recognised that the Tour had mushroomed beyond their organisational capacities.

1983

2,302 entrants
1,829 finishers
Men's winner: Robbie McIntosh 2:49:55
Women's winner: Heather Smithers 3:21:20

With over 2,000 entrants in all, this turned out to be year of the unconventional bikes. A tandem ridden by William Smith and Francois du Toit was fastest over a blustery and cool course, and Lloyd Wright had the third best time on one of the recumbent bikes for which he became famous (this one designed by John Stegmann). Wedged between them, the fastest conventional racer was local legend Robbie McIntosh, claiming his first of two Cycle Tour wins, only just shading the remarkable 47-year-old Don Spence and former champion Ertjies Bezuidenhout.

Running at UCT is active and going places! 1980 will be remembered as the year the club won two of the four UCT sports awards; Isavel Roche Kelly winning the Jamieson Cup for Sportsman of the Year and the 24-hour Relay Team the Landstem Trophy for Performance of the Year. A look back at 1980 shows an active year with many good performances.

24-Hour Relay

UCT — World University Record Holders! UCT's ten-man team raced to a World University record of 287 miles 672 yards in August, also bettering the previous year's S.A. club record by 2 miles 287 yards. Undoubtedly the highlight of the year, the UCT team raced mile after gruelling mile in a gutsy performance resulting in a team average of 5 mins a mile. No one should be singled out, but Chris Sole's average of 4 mins 40 secs for his 30 miles was a tremendous display of class. Chris has been the motivating force behind UCT's 24-hour relay successes over the last two years and UCT running in general over the last four years. He will not be at UCT in 1981 and his talent and enthusiasm will be greatly missed.

UCT also entered a B team which did well to come 8th out of the 26 teams, covering 262 miles 800 yards for a team average of 5 mins 28 secs a mile.

Athletics

Track and field, very weak for so long at UCT, came up with a bang in 1980. Early in the year Ricky Robinson and Chris Sole were performing consistently well, Ricky clocking a best time of 1.50,6 for the 800m and gaining selection for W.P. Dave Coutts-Trotter cleared 1,95 in the high jump to be selected for the W.P. U/19 team.

The start of the new season in the latter part of the year was marked by the appearance of a three lane grass track around the cricket oval and the appointment of Dave Welch as official UCT coach. Things started happening and UCT took third place in the Town League. Especially encouraging was the increasing participation by the women, in particular Anne Brodie, Cathy Fair, Denise Jones and Mandy Burgess.

Mark Halamandres ran an excellent 48,8 in the 400m, while Ricky Robinson and exciting new 'find' Greg Leifeldt ran 4.03 and 4.05 respectively for the mile at the Dream Mile Meeting at Coetzenberg in November. It would be tremendous if these two talented athletes could run sub 4 minute miles for UCT in the near future.

In November about twenty UCT athletes were in hard training for the SAU Athletics Champs in Durban which was to see the largest UCT contingent in years.

Opposite : Noel Hendricks, Peninsula Marathon 1980
Right : Isavel Roche-Kelly, Sportsman of the Year

Heather Smithers blew the women's record to 'Smithereens' by nearly 15 minutes.

> The most determined entrant was 13-year-old Kevin Hirons who rode from the start to his home in Fish Hoek, where he played a compulsory school rugby match, before completing his Tour in third last place.

ABOVE LEFT Theuns Mulder celebrates his 1984 win. He repeated the feat in the horror conditions of 1987.
ABOVE RIGHT The remarkably versatile Isavel Roche-Kelly, record-breaking champion of the Cycle Tour and Comrades.

1984

2,373 entrants
2,023 finishers
Men's winner: Theuns Mulder 2:55:07
Women's winner: Isavel Roche-Kelly 3:19:14

With a surname that combined the two great Irish names of world cycling, it's probably no surprise that Dublin-born UCT student Isavel Roche-Kelly sliced two minutes off the women's record for the Tour, but what is astounding is that, four years earlier, she had become the first women to ever win a silver medal in the Comrades Marathon, breaking the women's record for that event by more than an hour. Surely one of the most prestigious sporting doubles in the country's history. Sherianne Wolman was the first woman to cross the finishing line but Roche-Kelly had started later and won on corrected time. She was to die tragically young in a car accident.

In the men's event, the unheralded Theuns Mulder led from start to finish in a strong south-easter to defeat a host of more celebrated rivals. Yet another statistical landmark was achieved when more than 2,000 riders successfully completed the event.

ABOVE Swapping roles—the organiser of the 1985 Cycle Tour, John Wilmot, hits the road while his counterpart at the Two Oceans Marathon, Chet Sainsbury, takes to a bike.
ABOVE RIGHT The *Argus* coverage of the 1986 Tour, the first with 3,000 finishers.

1985

3,008 entrants
2,445 finishers
Men's winner: Hennie Wentzel 2:44:38
Women's winner: Louise van Riet Lowe 3:06:21

Records galore in perfect race conditions as the entries went past 3,000. Hennie Wentzel, winner in 1980, became the first man to win a second Cycle Tour, and he did it in record time. The 35-year-old was very much on home roads, and was seen as the grand old man of Western Province cycling. He would go on to win every Tour category except mountain bikes. The women's winner, Louise van Riet Lowe, went even better than 'Wiele', eclipsing the previous record by nearly 13 minutes.

Geoff Paxton from Johannesburg wrote himself into Cycle Tour folklore when his car broke down en route to Cape Town. Paxton simply unloaded his bike and cycled 10 km to Kroonstad to collect the necessary spares, and then pedalled back to repair his vehicle before carrying on in time to reach the start.

1986

3,494 entrants
3,086 finishers
Men's winner: Ertjies Bezuidenhout 2:40:20
Women's winner: Cathy Carstens 2:49:00

A highly controversial year in the Cycle Tour. Springbok team-mates Ertjies Bezuidenhout and Alan van Heerden crossed the finish line together with their arms linked in an attempt to create a dead-heat but they were foiled when, three days later, van Heerden was disqualified for 'being seconded from a moving vehicle'. Jonathan Heard, who had taken line honours in his unconventional bike, was also disqualified for 'failing to follow the instructions of a traffic officer, and unsafe riding'. All this left Bezuidenhout with his second Tour crown, and a new record time. But the real star of the show was the women's winner, Cathy Carstens, who had only taken up cycling one year before when injuries put paid to her running career. Her astounding winning time of 2:49:00 was the first under three hours, and put her within 10 minutes of the overall winner. Carstens would go on to win the event five times in a row and dominate South African women's road racing.

1987

5,934 entrants
4,761 finishers
Men's winner: Theuns Mulder 2:46:35
Women's winner: Cathy Carstens 3:03:24

The 10th anniversary Cycle Tour became the infamous Year of The Storm. It wasn't about winning; it was about surviving the worst conditions ever experienced on any Tour. The weather at the start—and for the first half of the race—was deceptively mild but, as the leaders passed the entrance to Cape Point, they were hit by a devastating cold wind and driving rain that, at times, brought slower competitors to a standstill or blew them off their bikes. Navy personnel carriers were deployed to collect miserable stragglers, and local radio stations broadcast appeals for locals with bakkies to assist as well. Many recall nervously going down the slippery hills slower than they went up. Remarkably, in spite of the truly horrendous weather (described in the *Argus* as 'Siberian'), 1,675 more riders managed to finish than had started the previous year. Theuns Mulder's second win was achieved in an extremely respectable 2:46:35, but even the redoubtable Cathy Carstens was blown back over three hours. Hennie Wentzel, who claimed line honours on a bike that was declared unconventional because of anti-wind fairings over the back wheel, said the conditions were so bad 'all I could see in front of me was a blur'.

One novice competitor, Neil Ballantyne, described 'going down the hill into Kommetjie in the pouring rain, brake levers touching the handlebars, brake cables as tight as banjo strings, and accelerating the whole time!'

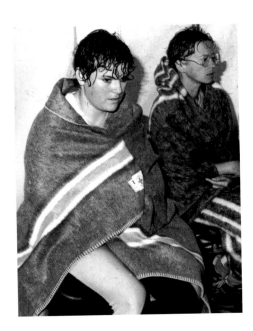

ABOVE A drenched Hennie Wentzel takes line honours in 1987 on a bike that was ruled unconventional. The tandem of Hans Degenaar and Pierre Smit is just behind.
LEFT The Arctic rains of 1987 provided the most demanding conditions yet experienced on the Cycle Tour.

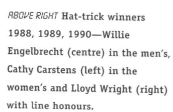

ABOVE RIGHT **Hat-trick winners 1988, 1989, 1990—Willie Engelbrecht (centre) in the men's, Cathy Carstens (left) in the women's and Lloyd Wright (right) with line honours.**

1988

10,850 entrants
8,707 finishers
Men's winner: Willie Engelbrecht 2:36:54
Women's winner: Cathy Carstens 2:54:23

This was the year the Cycle Tour entered the big league. In spite of, or maybe because of, the horror stories from the year before, entries almost doubled and leapt past 10,000, so that the start now occupied both sides of Hertzog Boulevard. M-Net provided the first television coverage of the event, and became a joint sponsor. The TV crews were caught napping, however, by the redoubtable Lloyd Wright who flashed around a windless course so fast in his specially imported recumbent that he had finished before they were ready. He was asked to repeat his finish for the benefit of the cameras. Willie Engelbrecht also took advantage of the favourable conditions to beat Steven Wolhuter, Mark Beneke and Robbie McIntosh in a blanket finish. Engelbrecht, probably the greatest of all male Cycle Tour competitors, would go on to notch up an unparalleled five wins.

1989

12,802 entrants
10,559 finishers
Men's winner: Willie Engelbrecht 2:49:24
Women's winner: Cathy Carstens 2:57:55

For the first time the organisers were forced to put a limit on the number of entries and, not for the last time, they found their prescribed envelope being pushed out. Only 12,000 were meant to start but somehow 12,802 got under way on a course that had been extended by 1 km to allow the finish to be at Maiden's Cove where, in theory, the authorities could better handle

the ever-increasing racing and spectating crowds. The extra 1,000 m meant little to the elite riders, but they added a small final climb that proved cruelly agonising for many slower competitors. It was another windy race day that produced markedly slower times, but otherwise it was an exact replica of the previous year—Lloyd Wright getting home first on his recumbent (in spite of 'nearly being blown off Chapman's Peak'), and Engelbrecht and Carstens taking the main racing honours.

ABOVE Faster than everyone: Lloyd Wright on his unconventional bike was first across the line four times.

1990

14,427 entrants
11,235 finishers
Men's winner: Willie Engelbrecht 2:41:56
Women's winner: Cathy Carstens 2:53:50

This was the first Cycle Tour in the new South Africa. The starting line was right beside the Grand Parade where, only eight weeks earlier, a massive, turbulent crowd had gathered to hear Nelson Mandela's speech after his release from prison. Momentous change was in the air, but the Tour went ahead with yet another record field, and Lloyd Wright, Willie Engelbrecht and Cathy Carstens completed a hat-trick of podium dominance. A massive pile-up at the bottom of Hospital Bend took down 50 riders, among them Lawrence Whittaker, who re-mounted and completed the Tour in spite of an injured arm. The results may have had a familiar look but the event was changing all the time—shifting to a Sunday, thereby allowing the police more scope to close roads, and helmets were made compulsory for the safety of all riders. Race packs were no longer posted to participants; they had to collect them at Camps Bay High School, and the resulting traffic bottlenecks prompted the future development of a separate Tour expo for registration, and to provide marketing opportunities for companies servicing the cycling community.

McIntosh reigns as main rivals crack

ABOVE Robbie McIntosh, back with a vengeance in 1991, was the first man under 2hrs 30.
BELOW King of the Road—Willie Engelbrecht, winner five times in seven years.

1991

15,593 entrants
12,750 finishers
Men's winner: Robbie McIntosh 2:28:46
Women's winner: Rene Scott 2:44:04

In perfect cycling conditions, Robbie McIntosh, eight years after his first victory, led a field of over 15,000 home and became the first rider ever to go under 2:30, in spite of riding solo from the foot of Suikerbossie. 'Mac the Knife' slashed more than 13 minutes off the conventional Tour record and over eight off Lloyd Wright's all-comers time. Springbok triathlete Rene Scott was no less impressive in the women's race, reducing Cathy Carstens' record by five minutes to a mark that still stands unchallenged. Commercially the Cycle Tour took two major leaps. Retail giant, Pick n Pay, committed to a substantial sponsorship relationship that has lasted 18 years to date, and the first expo and registration took place in the SA Maritime Museum in the Waterfront. Television coverage of the Tour received a boost when the 'Voice of Cycling', celebrated Tour de France commentator Phil Liggett, joined the M-Net team.

1992

17,274 entrants
13,334 finishers
Men's winner: Willie Engelbrecht 2:50:04
Women's winner: Jackie Martin 3:03:10

A hot and windy race day was not welcome news for the elite men, as the Cycle Tour had now become the final stage of the four day *Giro del Capo*. On tired legs, Willie Engelbrecht reclaimed his crown in a slow time, with Andrew McLean being the first overall *Giro* winner. Jackie Martin claimed the first of her three women's Cycle Tour wins. Throughout the field few personal bests were achieved, as the average finish time for the event literally blew out by an hour compared to the sublime conditions of the previous year. There was also a high percentage of dropouts.

1993

18,659 entrants
15,256 finishers
Men's winner: Wayne Burgess 2:33:35
Women's winner: Kim Carter 2:51:46

Wimpie van der Merwe, the runner-up in the very first Tour, achieved the fastest all-comers time ever on his recumbent—a breath-taking 2:16:40, which has not been breached since as interest in the unconventional bikes has waned. In the men's race, Wayne Burgess was the first amateur in 10 years, and the last, to win the Tour, but much of the attention in a fast race fell on second-placed Ilia Souprounov from Kazakhstan who became the first foreign rider to achieve a podium finish. The Tour had started to gather international momentum among pros and recreationals alike. Kim Carter took the women's title after a finish with Jackie Martin and Alta Kriegler that was so tight initially no one was sure who had triumphed. The LifeCycle Expo, as it was now known, moved across the Waterfront to A-Berth in Duncan Dock, and the smooth running of the entire event was a core feature of Cape Town's ultimately futile bid to host the 2004 Olympics.

1994

20,964 entrants
17,289 finishers
Men's winner: Willie Engelbrecht 2:23:22
Women's winner: Jackie Martin 2:49:19

With the country's first ever democratic elections only six weeks away, it would have been understandable if the Tour had taken a step back amidst the political tension but instead it surged relentlessly forward with what the *Argus* reported as 'a furiously ridden race'. For the first time entries exceeded 20,000 and clear, windless conditions allowed Willie Engelbrecht to experience what he described as 'the unbelievable high' of winning the race for the fifth time, and breaking the course record in the process. In all his Cycle Tour triumphs this was the only time Engelbrecht took line honours—he had been beaten to the finish by a tandem or unconventional in his previous victories. Over 5,000 riders went under 3:30 with the consistent Jackie Martin winning the women's race.

1995

25,313 entrants
20,535 finishers
Men's winner: Michael Andersson (Sweden) 2:22:56
Women's winner: Jackie Martin 2:45:52

Michael Andersson, the Super Swede, became the first-ever foreign winner of the Cycle Tour and, in another year of perfect race conditions, broke Engelbrecht's record in the process. Andersson also won the *Giro* and went on to record a respectable international career but, ultimately, he would be over-shadowed by the man he beat by one second—Kazakhstan's Alexandre Vinokourov. 'Vino' developed into one of the most exciting riders in world cycling, winning the 2006 Tour of Spain (the *Vuelta*) and finishing third behind Lance Armstrong in the 2003 Tour de France before suffering drug test humiliation in 2007. In the women's race, Jackie Martin defended her title and improved her personal best to within two minutes of Rene Scott's awesome 1991 record. The ever-present 'Wiele' Wentzel took the tandem race with his son Konrad. Entries once again surged dramatically, this time by 25%, and more than 20,000 riders finished the course within the cut-off time.

ABOVE the logistics of the 1993 Cycle Tour impressed the International Olympic Committee but not enough to win Cape Town the 2004 games. *Below* Michael Andersson edges out Alexandre Vinokourov in a high-class international finish in 1995

1996

28,711 entrants
22,294 finishers
Men's winner: Thomas Liese (Germany) 2:40:16
Women's winner: Erica Green 2:58:33

The German winner, Thomas Liese, was a former world champion who triumphed in the Cycle Tour in spite of setting out on 'a training ride for the Olympics', and then going on a solo break for the second half of the course. Back in the middle of the pack, cycling socially in a time of 3:31, was 50-year-old Belgian Eddy Merckx, five-times winner of the Tour de France, and viewed by many as the greatest cyclist ever. The then Premier of the Free State, Mosuioa Lekota, also took part accompanied by a biking bodyguard, and the field was sent on its way by the late Steve Tshwete, Minister of Sport. The Dutch pair of Henry Brokers and his blind partner, Jan Willem Mulder, won the tandem category in 2:51:21. Olympian Erica Green was the women's winner but, sadly, Jackie Martin didn't defend her crown after a training ride accident in Woodstock the day before the race.

The LifeCycle Expo and Registration moved to its current home at the Good Hope Centre, having completely outgrown the Waterfront.

ABOVE 1997 winner Norwegian Kurt Arvesen made it three foreign victories in a row. Robbie Hunter finished just behind him.

1997

28,875 entrants
22,717 finishers
Men's winner: Kurt Arvesen (Norway) 2:38:47
Women's winner: Erica Green 2:58:37

The 20th Tour took place in 'blessed weather' and unprecedented demand forced the organisers to relent on their original ceiling of 25,000. Kurt Asle Arvesen from Norway made it three in a row for foreign riders just nudging out Robbie Hunter, who would go on to become the first South African to ever compete in and win a stage of the Tour de France, and would claim a Cycle Tour win 10 years later. Erica Green retained her women's crown but she was no more than a bike-length ahead of runner-up, Port Elizabeth's Anriette Schoeman, who would win four consecutive Tours from 2000.

LEFT Malcolm Lange (on the right) wins by a wheel rim in 1998.
ABOVE Anke Erlank celebrates her first of four victories.

1998

34,162 entrants
25,955 finishers
Men's winner: Malcolm Lange 2:39:25
Women's winner: Anke Erlank 2:58:27

With close to 26,000 completing the race, the event was getting way beyond the capacity of the confines of the traditional finish area at Maiden's Cove. In changeable conditions, local rider Malcolm Lange broke the foreign domination of the men's race—but only just. In a blanket finish Lange got the nod by a fraction of a wheel. Anke Erlank topped a high-quality women's podium followed by Kim Carter, Anriette Schoeman and Erica Green (all former or future winners).

Has there ever been a more determined Cycle Tour competitor than Wiseman Bengo? Late in the afternoon of Saturday 7 March, 1998 Bengo, who is deaf, arrived on his bike at a Cape Town police station carrying a small bag and an application form for the Cycle Tour. He had cycled well over 1,000 km from his home in the Transkei to take part in the Tour. The police officers contacted Tour officials, who immediately made special late arrangements for Wiseman to take part. He completed the event in an impressive 3:34.

ABOVE Millenium champion Morné Bester salutes the crowd.

1999

36,153 entrants
28,885 finishers
Men's winner: Jacques Fullard 2:31:26
Women's winner: Michelle Lombardi 2:52:55

Jacques Fullard won what was to be the last of the 105 km Cycle Tours edging out German Jurgen Werner. The finish line remained at Maiden's Cove, but the Carnival moved to Green Point following a 5 km cool down ride—the twisting streets of Clifton and Bantry Bay were considered too dangerous for cycling in racing mode. Mountain bike champion Michelle Lombardi from Somerset West made a successful transition to the road, and took the women's title. All riders wore electronic timing transponders on ankle straps ending years of frustrating delays at the finish line.

An online entry system was available for the first time, but only for overseas entries.

2000

39,864 entrants
30,081 finishers
Men's winner: Morné Bester 2:39:35
Women's winner: Anriette Schoeman 2:57:34

The first of what would turn out to be four De-Tours. Fires and rock falls on Chapman's Peak forced the organisers to re-design their traditional route. Months of wrangling, mainly about the complete logistical isolation of Hout Bay that would result from any attempt to take the event through there, resulted in a Millennium Cycle Tour that was extended to 109 km, and skipped three of the most iconic sections of the race—Kommetjie and the climbs over Chappies and Suikerbossie. In their stead, the torturous 7 km ascent of Ou Kaapse Weg took the event to a new high, 75 m higher than Chapman's Peak, and produced some fearful anticipation among the recreational riders. Entries still reached record numbers and, for the first time, more than 30,000 finished. Ultimately most riders found the hair-raising, hair-pin descent from the tiring summit of Ou Kaapse Weg more concerning than the climb. The De-Tour came back into the city along the Blue Route and down Eastern Boulevard, providing a unique out-and-back effect, as the front-runners charged home past outgoing late starters before finishing at Green Point. Morné Bester set the benchmark time for the longer journey which, although it attracted all the professional riders, was no longer part of the *Giro* that now held its final stage on the day before the Cycle Tour. For the women, the Pocket Rocket Anriette Schoeman triumphed for the first time, and was never to be vanquished on the De-Tour.

2001

39,715 entrants
30,785 finishers
Men's winner: Douglas Ryder 2:31:57
Women's winner: Anriette Schoeman 2:55:21

Chappies remained closed after winter rains had dislodged more rocks onto the road and, with the extensive re-engineering that was necessary to make it safe yet to even begin, the De-Tour started to assume a permanent air. Online entries now exceeded 25,000 and a *Cape Argus* editorial described the event as 'one of the greatest mass sports spectacles in the world'. Capetonian Douglas Ryder took over seven minutes off the extended-course record, and won by no more than 50 cm from the Czech Tesar Lubor. Anriette Schoeman was chased home by former champion Kim Carter in the women's race. Mosuioa Lekota completed his fifth and final Cycle Tour, immediately offering his bike for sale at the finish. Cycle Tour legend Hennie Wentzel came in first in the tandems (with Mark Weedall), and then whipped around the course again, solo this time, in 3:45.

ABOVE Allan Davis becomes the first Australian to win the Tour in 2002.

2002

39,831 entrants
28,050 finishers
Men's winner: Allan Davis (Australia) 2:35:34
Women's winner: Anriette Schoeman 2:57:54

If 1987 was the Year of the Storm, then this was the Year of the Heat Wave. For the first and only time the Cycle Tour was closed down, as medical authorities feared for the safety of late riders in temperatures that soared on parts of the course to 42° (the weather forecast for the day had been 'fine and mild'!). Approximately 2,000 riders and their bikes were ferried to Green Point by trucks and buses after the route was shut at the foot of Ou Kaapse Weg at 14h45. Fire tenders were used for emergency supplies of water after it ran out at some drink stations, largely because frazzled riders were using the drinking water to give themselves a shower. The elite group, riding in the cool of the dawn, was led home by Australian Allan Davis. The women's race was swathed in controversy. Yet again Anriettte Schoeman crossed the line first but an unheralded Stellenbosch rider Ronel Liss claimed to have finished ahead of her, unnoticed. The prize-giving was put on hold whilst a special jury assessed the electronic timing reports. They could find no evidence that Liss had completed the entire course, and disqualified her.

ABOVE Cyclists load their bikes onto a truck in 2002 after the route was closed for late riders because of excessive heat.

 97

2003

39,668 entrants
27,841 finishers
Men's winner: Malcolm Lange 2:29:29
Women's winner: Anriette Schoeman 2:54:02

Mercifully mild conditions enabled Malcolm Lange to become the first man to go under 2:30 on the extended course. Lange had deliberately skipped the *Giro* to focus all his energies on winning a second Cycle Tour, five years after his first triumph. The irrepressible Anriette Schoeman saw off a big foreign challenge to make it four in a row, one short of Cathy Carstens' record. The Tour was delayed a week from its traditional second Sunday in March timeslot to accommodate the Cricket World Cup.

A brutal gust of wind blew all the towers in the start area down at 02h00 on race day. Some frantic repairs somehow ensured that everything looked shipshape by start time.

2004

42,614 entrants
31,219 finishers
Men's winner: Antonio Salomone (Italy) 2:32:23
Women's winner: Anke Erlank 2:49:23

Back to Chappies. After four years on the 'De-Tour', Chapman's Peak was finally open again—news that sparked a frenzy to take part in the 28th Cycle Tour with online entries opening and closing within three days. 40,000 entries were accepted in all. The Tour returned to its traditional path with two major exceptions. The organisers stretched the finish along the Atlantic Seaboard into Green Point by finding innovative ways to make the suburban streets of Bantry Bay and Sea Point safe for competitive racing, and, to retain the 109 km distance, they reluctantly excluded the scenic section through Kommetjie.

The return to Chappies was not without drama on a sweltering day, as one rider plummeted over the safety wall, and rock falls halted 2,500 backmarkers whilst the road was made safe but 31,219 riders successfully completed the race—the highest number to date.

Antonio Salomone headed a dramatic bunched sprint to win. He punctured 5 km from the finish but team-mate David George sacrificed his own wheel in the Italian's cause. 1998 winner Anke Erlank returned for her second triumph in a record-breaking women's race, stopping Anriette Schoeman's run of wins. Erlank broke away at Smitswinkel in a successful attempt to neutralise Schoeman's formidable sprinting talents.

Among the 1,697 international entrants were Frenchman Laurent Fignon and Spaniard Miguel Indurain, with seven Tour de France wins between them, both riding sedately with the Laureus Foundation group.

Going round more than once was the remarkable blind Dutch rider, Jan Mulder, and his sighted pilot Bart Boon who won the tandem section and then did a second lap in well under four hours. Mulder, a winner of three gold medals at the 2000 Paralympics, was competing in his 10th Tour.

Most Cycle Tour entrants were ecstatic about the return to Chappies, but Trevor Young didn't share their pleasure. On the tricky Klein Chappies descent he 'ran out of road' when his brakes failed to grip, crashing into and then over the retaining wall, plummeting 30 m down the cliff face. He suffered a fractured wrist and some abrasions.

ABOVE Italy's Antonio Salomone crosses the line in record time in 2004.

LEFT Blind rider Jan Mulder and his sighted pilot Bart Boon went round twice in 2004.
ABOVE Five times Tour de France winner Miguel Indurain takes it easy in the Cycle Tour pack.

ABOVE LEFT **England's Russell Downing beat the field and the wind in 2005.**
ABOVE CENTRE **Brilliant wheelchair athlete Ernst van Dyk took the inaugural Hand Cycle Race in the same year.**
ABOVE RIGHT **German Steffen Radochla triumphs in 2006. Nolan Hoffman (l) was second.**
BELOW **The Pocket Rocket, Anriette Schoeman, wins in 2006 equalling Cathy Carstens' record of five victories.**

2005

39,929 entrants
8,334 finishers
Men's winner: Russell Downing (England) 2:37:50
Women's winner: Anke Erlank 3:00:19

This year the south-easter really kicked in with gusts of well over 40 km/h recorded in places, and several riders literally blown off their bikes. Englishman Russell Downing, paced to the finish by his brother, recorded a respectable winning time, but Anke Erlank was forced to battle hard to become the first women's winner in 13 years to exceed three hours. Four-times defending champion Anriette Schoeman lost her chance of another title in a crash on the Blue Route. Five-times winner Cathy Carstens also fell on Klein Chappies, and local favourite David George came short in the hectic sprint finish of a race that was, once again, ridden as the final stage of the *Giro*.

A new two-stage entry system was introduced, replacing the first-come-first-served method of the past. Entrants who met certain cycling criteria were now given preference. For the first time the start was broadcast live by SABC, and a further new development was the Hand Cycle Race, won by top ranked wheelchair athlete Ernst van Dyk in 3:21:10.

2006

40,064 entrants
28,818 finishers

Men's winner: Steffen Radochla (Germany) 2:34:28
Women's winner: Anriette Schoeman 2:59:08

Cool weather and light rain resulted in a fast Tour, the average speed being 10 minutes quicker than the previous year. German Steffen Radochla was swiftest of all and, following Thomas Liese 10 years earlier, was the second winner from Leipzig. Runner-up Nolan Hoffman was the first black cyclist to get a podium finish. Anriette Schoeman recorded her fifth women's win in a time of 2:59:08 but treasured it more than her others because it was her first over the traditional Chappies route.

2007

41,279 entrants
30,095 finishers
Men's winner: Robbie Hunter 2:32:36
Women's winner: Anke Erlank-Moore 2:48:29

A calm, misty day for the 30th Tour delivered perfect conditions for South Africa's premier road racer, Robbie Hunter, to finally claim a Cycle Tour crown. Hunter, who first rode the Tour 20 years earlier as a 10-year-old, returned from his Italian base to outsprint defending champion Steffen Radochla. Later in the year Hunter was to achieve an even more memorable triumph for his Barloworld team when he won a stage of the Tour de France. Anke Erlank-Moore, riding on 'fantastic legs', took her fourth women's title in a longer course record without serious challenge from her rival Anriette Schoeman, who competed with a broken wrist in a cast. Around 20 cyclists were injured in a spectacular pile-up on the notorious Hospital Bend, which caused a 30-minute delay for later starters.

ABOVE LEFT **South Africa's premier road racer Robbie Hunter finally triumphs in 2007.**
ABOVE **Queen again. Anke Erlank-Moore reclaims her crown in 2007.**

Greg LeMond and Jan Ullrich brought to five the number of Tour de France winners who have ridden the Cycle Tour, and international entries exceeded 2,000.

Cape Argus Editor Chris Whitfield rode with his youngest daughter, Robynne, completing a full house of tandem Tours, having previously ridden with his wife and his two other daughters.

All of the Magnificent Seven—Neil Bramwell, Louis de Waal, Steph du Toit, Gareth Holmes, Stephen Stefano, Alex Stewart and Neville Yeo—completed the full house of 30 Cycle Tours. First of them home was the 'youngster', 43-year-old Stefano (3:27) who was only 13 when he took part in the inaugural Tour.

A unique tandem combination was former Springbok captain Francois Pienaar and former Bafana Bafana skipper Lucas Radebe who confessed the experience was tough, saying 'there's nowhere to hide in cycling'. They were riding for Pienaar's MAD (Make A Difference) Foundation. Also riding from a different sporting discipline was tennis great Johan Kriek who brought five American friends to enjoy the experience and to raise funds for charity.

30 YEARS OF WINNERS

	1978	1979	1980	1981	1982	1983	1984	1985	1986	1987	1988	1989	1990	1991	1992
No of entrants	525	999	1,398	1,669	1,698	2,302	2,373	3,008	3,494	5,934	10,850	12,802	14,427	15,593	17,274
No of finishers	446	760	1,119	1,372	1,347	1,829	2,023	2,445	3,086	4,761	8,707	10,559	11,235	12,750	13,334
Men's winner	L Whittaker	JJ Degenaar	H Wentzel	E Bezuidenhout	M Pinder	R McIntosh	T Mulder	H Wentzel	E Bezuidenhout	T Mulder	W Engelbrecht	W Engelbrecht	W Engelbrecht	R McIntosh	W Engelbrecht
Time	3:02:25	2:52:28	3:02:18	2:47:42	3:01:25	02.49.55	02.55.07	02:44:38	2:40:20	02:46:35	02.36.54	02:49:54	02:41:56	2:28:46	02:50.04
Women's Winner	J Theis	J Theis	S Broekhuyzen	A Wood	M le Roux	H Smithers	I Roche-Kelly	L v Riet Lowe	C Carstens	C Carstens	C Carstens	C Carstens	C Carstens	R Scott	J Martin
Time	4:35:00	3:36:46	03.51.00	3:40:01	3:34:54	3:21:20	3:19:14	3:06:21	2:49:00	3:03:24	2:54:23	2:57:55	2:53:50	2:44:04	03.03.10
First tandem	J & R Stegmann	J & R Stegmann	J & R Stegmann	F & A du Toit	F du Toit/ W Smith	F du Toit/ W Smith	F du Toit/ W Smith	A Macdonald/ J Heard	G Hall/ P Callow	H Degenaar/ P Smit	F du Toit/ B Mostert	A Macdonald/ G Genis	C van Zyl/ G Hall	I Buratovich/ M Blewett	R Chesterton/ C van Zyl
Time	4:15:00	3:52:00	3:29:00	3:07:10	3:08:11	2:41:46	2:48:17	2:43:12	2:46:58	2:43:06	2:40:32	2:49:41	2:42:30	2:37:01	2:49:42
Unconventional line honours							L Wright			H Wentzel	L Wright	L Wright	L Wright		
Time							02:43:51			02:43:05	02:33:03	02:37:35	02:40:29		

CONTINUED	1993	1994	1995	1996	1997	1998	1999	2000	2001	2002	2003	2004	2005	2006	2007
No of entrants	18,659	20,964	25,313	28,711	28,875	34,162	36,153	39,864	39,715	39,831	39,668	42,614	39,929	40,064	41,279
No of finishers	15,256	17,289	20,535	22,294	22,717	25,955	28,885	30,081	30,785	28,050	27,841	31,219	28,334	28,818	29,296
Men's winner	W Burgess	W Engelbrecht	M Andersson	T Liese	K Arvesen	M Lange	J Fullard	M Bester	D Ryder	A Davis	M Lange	A Salomone	R Downing	S Radochla	R Hunter
Time	02.33.05	2:23:22	2:22:56	2:40:16	2:38:47	2:39:25	2:31:26	2:39:35	2:31:57	2:35:34	2:29:59	2:32:23	2:37:50	2:34:28	2:32:36
Women's Winner	K Carter	J Martin	J Martin	E Green	E Green	A Erlank	M Lombardi	A Schoeman	A Schoeman	A Schoeman	A Schoeman	A Erlank	A Erlank	A Schoeman	A Moore (Erlank)
Time	2:51:46	2:49:19	2:45:52	2:58:33	2:58:37	2:58:27	2:52:55	2:57:34	2:55:21	2:57:29	2:54:02	2:49:23	3:00:19	2:59:08	2:48:29
First tandem	I Buratovich/ K Gaynor	A de Kock/ H Botes	O Stielau/ T Roolvink	J W Mulder/ H Brokers	H Wentzel/ M Weedall	H Wentzel/ M Weedall	S Richardson/ M Welgemoed	S Richardson/ M Welgemoed	H Wentzel/ M Weedall	J Brittan/ B Moore	A McLean/ C Germs	J Mulder/ B Boom	G & M Beneke	C Botha/ P Schoeman	C Botha/ P Schoeman
Time	2:45:14	2:41:26	2:35:08	2:51:22	2:48:01	2:51:48	2:40:40	2:52:23	2:48:13	2:56:32	2:50:35	2:44:40	2:50:24	2:48:46	2:38:20
Unconventional line honours	W van der Merwe														
Time	02:16:40														

The celebrities

ABOVE LEFT Tourism Minister Mohammed Valli Moosa in the saddle.

ABOVE RIGHT Archbishop Desmond Tutu gets in some training with former *Cape Argus* Editor Moegsien Williams but sadly the Nobel Peace Prize winner didn't compete.

LEFT Radio man Alex Jay tries to enjoy himself.

OPPOSITE A new ball game for cricketer Paul Adams (top left), tennis star Johan Kriek (top right), rugby's Francois Pienaar and football's Lucas Radebe (on the tandem).

THE ODDITIES

Cycle Tour co-founder John Stegmann saw the development of 'any human-powered vehicles' as a key part of the event. He rode tandems himself, and designed unconventional vehicles for others to ride, and the category trophy for the Tour still bears his name.

Often the unusual creations finished in front of, or right among, the top registered solo racers, causing celebration for their inventors and some frustration and confusion for serious cycling enthusiasts. Lloyd Wright led the Cycle Tour home four times on various recumbents including the famous occasion in 1988 when he had finished so fast in his American import, named The Lightning after a World War II fighter-bomber, that he caught the television cameras unawares, and had to repeat the final leg for their benefit. In the high winds often experienced on the Tour it takes plenty of courage, as well as skill and stamina, to pilot the unconventionals, and even someone as skilled as Wright was literally blown out of the race in 1987.

The category reached its peak in 1993 when Wimpie van der Merwe completed the course in a record 2:16:40, which still stands, and swept past the *Giro* pros at Kommetjie even though he had started 15 minutes after them.

Since then interest has waned a little in the 'funny bikes' although they can still be found on the road every year.

Now it's more a case of 'funny riders', as the Tour continues to attract an astonishing array of costumes and tandem combinations. I cycled virtually the entire 2003 Tour in the company of a man with an inflatable doll strapped to his back. He tried to repeat the experience the next year but it got blown off in a high wind at UCT, which must have provided a unique experience for the clean-up crew. I also cycled through Scarborough behind one cyclist dressed as the devil, who was riding alongside another entrant carrying a large banner proclaiming 'Praise God for All Things'. I can report that, alarmingly, the forces of evil began to pull ahead at Soetwater.

Some wear the uncomfortable costumes for charity or to raise awareness for a cause, others do it for fun, a bit of attention or, with luck, a few seconds of TV fame.

Undoubtedly it's a sure-fire way to get plenty of support from the crowd on the roadside but, above all, the extrovert characters remind everyone that the Cycle Tour is an event to be enjoyed.

ABOVE The recumbent riders often outpace the conventional pack.
OPPOSITE TOP Lloyd Wright, four times line honours' winner, in 'Lightning'.
OPPOSITE BELOW LEFT Wimpie van der Merwe rockets around the course in
an all-comers' record time in 1993.
OPPOSITE BELOW RIGHT Piloting a recumbent demands plenty of experience.

ABOVE On race day the Tour is run from the joint operations centre which co-ordinates
all emergency and administrative services.

BEHIND THE SCENES

The results of the first Cycle Tour were collated at a kitchen table in the home of one of the organisers. It took several days for the novice volunteers to sort out the admin from just over 500 riders.

Thirty years on, over 30,000 finishers are processed electronically and instantly, and a full-time Tour staff of eight is backed up by thousands of expertly mobilised people. The Cycle Tour has become a logistical phenomenon that has been studied by foreign event organisers, and was used as a best-practice model for the Cape Town 2004 Olympic Bid.

It now costs in excess of R14m to run each year, and generates R4m in funding for its joint beneficiaries, Pedal Power and Rotary.

The event is owned by the specially created Cape Town Cycle Tour Trust designed to resolve long-standing strains between Pedal Power, which founded the event, and Rotary, which took over the operational management in 1982 as the event grew well beyond the spare-time capacities of the founders and their helpers.

Pedal Power devotes most of its Tour funds to development cycling and the promotion of safer cycling in general, trying to raise the profile of the sport across all racial groups. Rotary spreads its revenue across a range of community initiatives. In 2007 these included crèches in Mitchell's Plain, the Ncedeluntu Sanctuary for abandoned children, the SA Guide Dogs Association, the Sarah Fox Hospital, the Mustadafin Foundation, and supplying computers and bikes to Ocean View High School, which lies on the route.

The Cape Town Cycle Tour Trust formally manages the Tour but it sub-contracts some responsibilities to Rotary clubs and other service organisations. Over 2,500 volunteers are involved on race day.

As two-thirds of the route runs through a national park and world heritage site, a key part of the Tour's success is its environmental management plan which looks at every possible environmental impact the event could have – litter, noise pollution, helicopter flight paths, fire risks, wildlife disturbance, traffic management and structural safety en route.

The Cycle Tour was the first cycling event in the world to incorporate such a comprehensive environmental management plan, and the International Cycling Union now requires all events under its auspices to have a similar one.

The aim of the organisers is to clear the 65 cubic metres of rubbish generated by the Tour's 35,000 riders and their supporters within 36 hours, and to recycle at least 70 per cent of it. The task is not made any easier by modern sachets of energy gel that stick to the road like glue, and attract crowds of hungry baboons that then block traffic for hours!

ABOVE **Stalwart Cycle Tour administrator Pat White swamped with applications in the days before online bookings.**

ABOVE *Cape Argus* Editor Chris
Whitfield (left), Cycle Tour
Sponsorship & Marketing Director
David Bellairs (centre) and
Raymond Ackerman, Chairman
of Pick n Pay, celebrate another
successful Cycle Tour.
OPPOSITE More than 9,000 bikes
are flown into and out of Cape
Town International Airport for
the Cycle Tour.

The final stretch of the race from Camps Bay through to Green Point represents a special engineering challenge. Four pedestrian bridges have to be constructed from 04h00 on race day, and be certified as safe before the first riders come through. And then they have to be completely dismantled within two hours of the final cyclists passing by to allow heavy vehicles back on the road.

The Tour's joint operations centre, which integrates all the various emergency and Tour management services on race day, is considered to be one of the best of its kind, running a complex operation that must also cater for the needs of the communities cut off by road closures. The medical staff monitors weather conditions with a sophisticated demand model that, for instance, predicted serious and possibly critical water shortages during the heat wave of 2002, and compelled the closure of the event for the late riders. Twenty buses and extra tankers of water are on stand-by for such crises.

The consumption statistics of the Tour are daunting. At the 18 refreshment stations 50,000 ℓ of Powerade, 160,000 ℓ of Coca-Cola, 100,000 ℓ of water, 50,000 kg of ice and 450,000 paper cups are used (it's a source of great pride to the organisers that they persuaded the Atlanta giant for the first time anywhere to stop waxing those paper cups so that they could be recycled). And it was estimated in 1998 that the amount of Coke drunk during the Cycle Tour would fuel a small car to drive from the Cape to Cairo 128 times.

ABOVE **Winning Time, specialists in event timing, digitally record every participant through key points on the course.**
ABOVE RIGHT **The Tricycle Tour— just one of many events in LifeCycle Week which now surrounds the Tour.**

All that input demands an output, and there are 134 portaloos around the course, and more than 3,000 rolls of toilet paper are used on race day. One very windy year, when some of the toilets in the start area were blown into the road, the organisers drolly noted new levels of service—where the facilities went to the riders, rather than the other way round.

Off the bike, the Tour has become a serious business as well. The Lifecycle Expo and Registration has become the biggest of its kind in the country. The idea of a registration centre to bring entrants together, create a vibe, and generate commercial opportunity was taken from the Comrades. The first effort in 1990 involved about six stands at the Camps Bay High School, and caused monumental traffic jams in the area. It moved to the Waterfront before reaching its current home, the Good Hope Centre.

The Expo is now part of LifeCycle Week, which involves a rapidly growing mountain bike challenge at Boschendal, a tricycle tour, and a special juniors event all coinciding with the professional action of the *Giro del Capo*. The Tour organisers also appoint 15 seeding events around the country during the year to allow riders to improve their start times. Those races need to be spread far and wide because less than half the entrants to the Tour come from the Cape. Airlines have to lay on special shipping arrangements for the many thousands of bikes that are increasingly coming in from abroad as well. Over 2,000 foreign entries were received in 2007, including 537 from the UK, 385 from Namibia and 182 from Germany.

The youngest riders to complete the Cycle Tour have been six-years-old, and the oldest is the irrepressible Japie Malan at 88 years and 8 months. The average age of the men in 2007 was 40 and for the women, who made up roughly one-fifth of the field, it was 37. The average time for the men was a shade above four hours, for the women it was 4:42.

The business of the Cycle Tour never ends. Each year's race is followed by a substantial administrative wrap-up and numerous de-brief and analysis sessions. Preparation for the next race begins immediately, as over 40,000 prospective entrants will be online in September trying to secure their places. A Partners' (sponsors) workshop is held in August to structure all the commercial opportunities for the year ahead. The Rotarian volunteer operation is now a smooth-running machine, but it demands constant planning and activity.

But it's a mistake to reduce the Cycle Tour and its organisation to mechanics and statistics. There is an extraordinary spirit that has spread through a couple of generations of Tour employees, administrators, volunteers, sponsors and city officials. Behind the scenes most will admit that it's not always been plain sailing on an ocean of goodwill but, somehow, every year for 30 years, the event has delivered a remarkable experience for the cyclists and the city.

Whether motivated by a passion for cycling, community service, professionalism, or a sense of civic pride, the people who have grown the Tour over the past 30 years can stand tall. They have built something very special.

ABOVE LEFT **Underprivileged kids getting their wheels from the funds Pedal Power raises from the Cycle Tour.**
ABOVE **Volunteers in all shapes and sizes have been the key to the Tour's success.**

OPPOSITE TOP LEFT The Cycle Tour's oldest
competitor Japie Malan, 88.
OPPOSITE TOP RIGHT Cycle Tour Event
Planning & Management Director Ken
Sturgeon hands out computers funded
by the Tour at Ocean View School.
OPPOSITE BELOW The special pedestrian
bridge over Beach Road in Sea Point,
assembled and dismantled in less
than a day.
ABOVE & RIGHT The 18 refreshment stations
pump out liquids and music all day long.

The camaraderie

Cycle Tour Good Samaritan stories abound but one of the most remarkable was recorded in 1996. Nineteen-year-old Carmen Gold lost her pedals 1km from the start, and was walking forlornly in the hope of help—which arrived in the form of Adenaan Loofer, who had started too fast and was already cramping. Loofer, believing he had no chance of completing the Tour, gave Gold his bike, and offered to walk hers back to the start area. As he walked, he encountered an unidentified woman who was struggling with her bike chain and he helped her fix the problem. By then she was too discouraged to continue and gave her bike to Loofer, whose cramps had now vanished. He accepted the kind offer and completed the course. Somehow all three bikes ended up back with their rightful owners.

ABOVE **The Magnificent Seven who have completed every Cycle Tour—from left Gareth Holmes, 49, Neil Bramwell, 69, Stephen Stefano, 43, Steph du Toit, 59, Louis de Waal, 69, Alex Stewart, 68, Neville Yeo, 60.**

Gareth Holmes is deaf 'I can't hear and I can't talk with the rest of the bunch so it can be dangerous'; Neil Bramwell is the oldest of them and has served as Chairman of Pedal Power; Stephen Stefano is the youngest and rode his first 16 Tours on a bike he won in a lucky draw at the Ride-In demonstration that led to the establishment of the Cycle Tour; Steph du Toit's handlebar broke at Soetwater in 1998 but he managed to tape it together and keep his ever-present record intact; Louis de Waal wore number 001 in the first Tour and has contributed enormously to cycling administration ever since; Alex Stewart's bike has never broken and he's not even had a puncture in 30 years; Neville Yeo rode the 1987 Year of the Storm Tour with his 10-year-old son and is still trying to beat the three hour mark for the first time.

THE MAINSTAYS—
FIFTEEN TOURS OR MORE

Most Cycle Tour entrants return for another year and many keep on returning year after year. Seven have completed all 30 Tours to date and over 1,800 have the honour of finishing at least 15 times.

30 TOURS

Bramwell	Neil
de Waal	Louis
du Toit	Stephanus F
Holmes	Gareth
Stefano	Stephen
Stewart	Alex
Yeo	Neville

29 TOURS

Booth	Trevor
Jack	Josef
Maggott	Selwyn
Smith	Dennis
van der Velde	Frank

28 TOURS

Gasson	Barrie
Hemp	Angus
Hinrichsen	Trevor
Jacobs	Kenneth Brian
Kagan	Selwyn
Lakay	David
Louw	Johan
Milner	Charles Mordaunt
Schafer	Norman
van Rooy	Darrell Mervyn
van Wyk	Charles Martin

27 TOURS

Bales	Peter
Brousseau	Ferdinand Martin
Ciapparelli	Sergio
Degenaar	Johannes Jacobus
Deuchar	Alexander John
Eastman	Bruce
Ferguson	Gus
Fish	Robert
Jenkins	Stephen James
Malherbe	Gideon
Michel	Bernard
Minter	Keith
Nixon	Denis
Pinder	Mark
Viljoen	Marko Jacobus
Vreulink	Bernard
Wilmot	John

26 TOURS

Adams	Frederick
Anderson	Timothy William
Arendse	Stanford
Ashley	Keith
Brown	Colin Thomas
Cloete	Claude George
Howe	Tony
Huckle	Colin William
Jacobs	Solomon
Jacobs	Stephen Bradley
Jones	Arnie
Kensley	Peggi
Loubser	Johannes Tobias
McDonald	Neil
Schafer	Karl-Heinz
Smith	Izak
Smith	John Henry
Stevens	John
Woodhead	Stuart
Wright	Lloyd Bernard

25 TOURS

Basson	Olga
Boardman	Tom
Cammidge	Mark
Carew	Clive
Dear	Kenneth
Dutkiewicz	Colin
Edwards	Errol
Frouws	Louis
Krohn	Wilfried
Kropman	Gerard Anthony
Mannix	Brian
McInnes	Ian Philip
Reid	William James
Salo	Leslie
Shield	Trevor
Stephenson	John
Symington	Paul Leslie
Thomlinson	Edward
Viljoen	Francois

24 TOURS

Bergh	Neil
Boardman-Smith	Warren
Clarence	Russell
Driver-Jowitt	Jon
du Plessis	Armand Morné
du Plooy	Barry Michiel
Everson	George
Frazer	James
Genis	Gerard
Hammar	Dennis
Hemp	Marjorie
Hinrichsen	Gina

Hodgkinson	Peter Dayton
Howes	Philip
Jeftha	Desmond Henry William
Langley	George Bernard
Latimer	Mick
Leahy	John
Leaver	Roy
Leeson	Mario
Melck	Michael
Milner	Marcus
Moss	Janet
Muzik	Petr
Putterill	David Kenneth Murdoch
Smuts	Petrus Gerhardus
Spreckley	Terence
Swiel	Robin Lindsey
Thompson	Ronald Stuart
Torr	Clive
Unite	David
Wheeldon	Andrew Murray
Wheeler	Peter-John Haven

23 TOURS

Barker	Willy
Basson	Attie
Boonzaier	Neil
Cartwright	Tim
Clarke	Richard
Colussi	Lorenzo
Cope	Alvin
Cope	Dennis
Doherty	Peter Derek
Eloff	John Pierre
Fisher	John
Freeman	Kenneth John
George	Chris
Gomm	Robert
Greveling	Jeroen
Gurney	Keith
Hemp	Jonathan
Hermann	Neil Henry
Herring	Robert
Hill	N S
Howe	Margaret
Kantor	Shirley
Kroezen	Michael John
Krohn	Penny
Lipshitz	Noel
Lizzi	Elaine
Mandy	Derek
Meiring	Stan
Milner	Patrick

Moss	John
Pey	Claus-Dieter
Rhodes	Malcolm
Roberts	Trygve Sante
Salie	Ismaiel
Scott	Cameron Bruce
Sinclair	Ian
Slabber	Martin J
Sulter	Brennan
Swoboda	Marie Louise
van der Spuy	Melody May
Viljoen	Hercules Stephanus
Whittaker	Lawrence
Williams	Denny
Wilmot	Tanja
Zylstra	Xavier

22 TOURS

Abrahams	Leon Gary
Barlow	Lynn Anthony
Barson	Brian
Benningfield	Brian
Bentley	Steven
Boltman	Chris A
Bradburn	Ian
Brettenny	Malcolm
Buchholtz	Graham
Busse	Anthony Eric
Cohen	Martin
Correia	Jose
de Kock	Alwyn
de Rooy	Klaas
Dippenaar	André
Early	Don
Gresele	Ivan
Hain	Wilfrid
Hopkins	Kenneth Thomas
Howell	Michael

Jegger	Robert	D'Aguiar	Larry	Melck	Hilary	Correia	Humberto
Kriel	Jonathan Calf	Davids	Abdul Quayum	Miller	Duncan James	Crozier	Michael John
Madison	Shaun	de Villiers	Timothy	Mosca	Giovanni	Daniel	Craig
Mallinson	Noel John Vaughan	Dewar	Kevin Neale	Muller	Gunter	Davidowitz	Michael
Marnitz	Wolfgang	Dixon	K Y P	Murphy	Richard	de Jager	Desiree Geesje
McEvoy	John Michael	Doney	Robin	Pearson	Brian	Dose	Alexander Gordon
McGill	John	du Toit	Aletta	Pettit	Terence George	du Plooy	Thomas
Meaker	Paul	Evans	Leon Roy	Pogrund	Ivan Barry	du Toit	Leon
Miranda	Manuel	Evertson	Deavoleen	Pomario	Robert	Dunwell	Michael
Quevauvilliers	Noel Gilles	Fitt	Dean	Procter	Alan	Dyer	Norman Douglas
Romanes	Lyle	Friebus	Charles Edward	Proctor	Peter	Erlangsen	Keith Robert
Roux	Philip	Gallard	Ian	Raimondo	Frank Emilio	Fagan	Henry Allan
Rutherford	Paul Leslie	Galloway	David	Ranger	Kevin	Fiedler	Guenther
Schell	Clive	Gericke	Johann	Romanovsky	Gerald	Forbes	Gordon
Stein	Michael	Goldblatt	Lance	Ryder	Douglas	Francis	Bernard
van der Linden	Carel Marinus	Goodall	Pat	Sacker	Darin	Freeman	Diane Anita
van Heerden	Alan	Gouws	Vincent	Sanby	James	Futter	Bradley
van Jaarsveld	Albertus Stephanus	Greeff	Awie	Schildt	Bjorn	Gamble	Raymond
van Velden	Johannes	Greveling	Tjeerd	Schmidt	Reinhard	Garai	Charles
Walker-Wells	Keith	Haupt	Peter	Schutters	Sharrell Louie	Geater	Les
Wiehman	Jan	Herren	Hans	Selman	Robert James	Geldenhuys	Lee-Roy
Woodburn	Don	Hettasch	Hans Bernhard	Shapiro	Steve	Gibbons	Graham John
Zoomers	Nicolaas	Horsfield	Michael	Siefe	Dario	Greeff	Hennie
		Ireland	Brian	Sissons	John	Griffiths	Dave

21 TOURS

				Smith	Andrew Henry	Grobler	Garth
Avnit	Dave	Jacobs	Albertus	Stegmann	John	Haden Smith	Robert
Bailey	Lance Raymond	Jacobs	Kevin Robert	Strubing	Dieter	Herron	Raif
Barber	Peter John	Jankelow	Ralph	Struthers	Walter	Howell	Anthony Neville
Basson	Jacques	Kilbey	Graham Ranger	Sturgeon	Kenneth Bryan	Jacobs	Stanley
Basson	Paul	Koning	Paul	Sumner	Linda	Jooste	Lowell
Becker	Greg	Kuiper	Vivian	Swil	Tony	Keen	Gustaf Anthony
Berry	Carina	Kuun	Johan	Sylvester	Mark Gavin	Kelly	Peter
Brand	John	Landman	Venetia	Terry	Arnot Hendrik	Koekemoer	Johannes Gerhardus
Brink	Tim	le Grange	Eddie	Thring	Tom	Kramer	Peter Adriaan
Broeksma	Reitz	le Roux	Jacques Frederick	Tully	James	Lamond	Peter
Burger	Damien	Linde	Dirk	van Andel	Herman	Levy	Fred
Carmohn	Erik	Lindenberg	Graeme	van der Linde	Phillip	Lill	Bevan
Carr	Garnet John	Long	David Stephen	van der Linde	Vernon William	Loveland	Peter
Coetze	Andries Christiaan Petrus	Lotter	Ras	van der Linden	Els	Mallinson	Judy Margaret
Coetzee	Albert	Loubser	Dante	van Rensburg	Almore	McGavin	Ian Gerald
Colbeth	Gary	Macdonald	Alastair Gray	van Zyl	Noel Andrew	McKie Thomson	Campbell
Counsell	Clarence Hilary	Masters	Nicholas	Volkwyn	Charles	McMahon	John
Crawford	Elaine	Matthee	Friedrich Wr	Wentzel	Hennie	Mitchell	Jonathan
Creed	Anthony Gerald	McCoy	Sean	Wilson	Peter	Mostert	Berty
		McEwan	Leslie Graham	Wiseglass	Philip Larry	Muller	Dirk
				Wright	John	Naude	André
				Zink	Linda Renee	Noble	Ryland Winton
				Zink	Philip John	O'Regan	Arthur Stephen

20 TOURS

Abrahams	Ebrahim	Parker	Henry
Aginsky	Rael	Pentz	Marc
Anderson	Peter Durant	Petrie	John Ian
Barbe	John Edward Gerard	Pickering	John
Beamish	Julie	Pieret	Joy
Bester	Robert	Plath	Peter
Bird	Colin Clive	Procter	Marita
Blignaut	Calie	Rabinowitz	Meyer
Brown	Alistair	Robertson	Alexander
Brummer	Nick	Saxe	Maon Steven
Burton	Robin Michael	Schonegevel	James
Carmichael-Green	Mark	Smit	Johan
Childes	Michael Patton	Smit	Tappies
Cilliers	Adriaan Michiel	Stander	Melchior J
Cohen	Mark	Stuart	Graham Murray
Collins	Pieter J	Taylor	Tony Robert Charles
		Thiart	Gerrie
		Thomson	Deven Frank

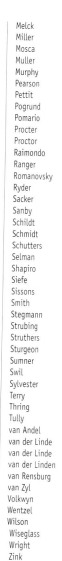

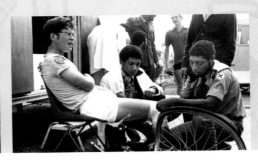

van den Berg — John Mauritz
van der Spuy — Philip Charl
van der Westhuizen — Dennis Mark
van Heerden — Conrad
van Onselen — Linus
Wait — John
Walters — Shirley Carol
Welthagen — Chris
Wiggins — Spencer
Woodin — Ron
Wraight — John
Wright — Andrew Ernest
Zeidel — Hymie

19 TOURS

Abitz — Asher
Abrahams — André
Abrahamse — Brent
Abrahamson — Ian
Adam — Ted
Andrew — Neil Spencer
Andrew — Roy
Baker — Michael
Balharry — Graham Robb
Barker — Christopher
Barker — Rosy
Becker — Simon
Benjamin — Paul Cedric
Berger — Simon
Berry — Patrick
Bishop — Lawrence
Borel-Saladin — Carle Jean Leon
Bothner — Charles
Brass — Stephen
Breuninger — Heinrich Karl
Brits — Philip
Brits — Theunis
Brown — Guy Lawrence
Brownell — Geoff
Bruce — Jeremy
Burton — Robert
Chesterton — Richard
Clarke — David Alan
Colyn — Barry
Conradie — Gerrit
Cowgill — Vanessa
Crook — Roger
Dallimore — Brian
Daniels — Shaun
de Haast — Eef
de Kock — Andrew

de Villiers — Francois
Denton — Louwie
dos Santos — Amilcar Alves
Draaijer — Atie
Dreyer — Douglas
du Plessis — Philip
du Toit — Christopher
du Toit — Reline
du Toit — Willem Anton
Dwyer — Frank
Eave — David
Faure — Ken
Fillmore — John
Gertze — Gregory
Gibbs — James Boyd
Glaum — Martin
Greeff — Johan
Griffiths — Cheryl
Hagberg — Gordon James
Halliday — Barry
Handler — Leonard
Hardy — Tony
Hart — Ian
Hartzenberg — Mark
Heald — Basil Gary
Hodson — Alan
Holgate — Mark
Jamneck — Gerrus
Jansen van Vuuren — Shane
Johnston — David
Johnston — Derrick Kevin
Jonker — Martin
Jordaan — Etienne
Keen — Alan
Kensley — Ken
Keppler — Ivor
Knowles — Jane
Koopman — Frank
Kratz — Rolf
Laubscher — Ferdinand
Lea — Robert Patrick
Lewis — Mike Arundel
Lincoln — Marc
Louw — Eugene
Maartens — Jo
Maclear — Gary
Margolin — Issy
McLean — Andrew Richard
McLeod — William
McMaster — Clive
Meiring — Pieter Jan

Meyer — Detlef Ernst Herbert
Miller — Raoul Paul
Mills — Richard Alexander
Moore — Heather
Morris — Stuart Grant
Mottalini — Giovanni Rodolfo
Nixon — John Brian
Ould — David
Pearson — Lynne
Petzer — Mark
Phelp — David Thomas
Potgieter — Erik
Pretorius — Erasmus Jacobus P
Prinsloo — Shaun Martin Albert
Rex — John Alan
Rix — Patricia Merle
Robinson — Kenneth
Rosingana — Mario Francesco
Rowan-Parry — Lynne
Rowles — Hugh
Sayers — Mark
Schaffer — Mervyn
Searle — John
Sendin — William
Sirin — Avron
Smith — Rodney John
Smulders — Ronald
Steffen — August
Stein — Barry
Stemmet — Johannes Daniel
Stern — Ivor
Stokoe — Clive
Stone — Richard Georg
Swanepoel — André
Swanepoel — Ronald
Tait — Mathew James
Taylor — Guy Latimer
Thornhill-Fisher — James
Tobiansky — Phillip J
van Assche — Daniel
van der Merwe — David
van der Mescht — Jan
van Esch — John
van Rhyn — Anthony Arnold
van Wyk — Johannes Frederikus
van Zyl — Marius
van Zyl — Paul Pischinger
Virgin — Robert George Spencer
Vlok — Louis
Vlok — Morkel
Vosloo — André

Vreulink — Anton
Walser — Dietmar
Webb — Mark
White — Graham
Willows — Desmond Kenneth
Windvogel — Bertram
Wolhuter — Wollie
Wolmarans — Tjaart N

18 TOURS

Absalom — Johannes J
Ackermann — Jack
Attwood — Creslin
Ball — Bob
Beneke — Gary
Beugelink — Ben
Beukes — Wessel
Blignaut — Anne
Borman — Henry
Brass — Julie
Brink — Jacobus Theunis Briers
Brits — Gerhard
Brodovcky — Hertzel
Brouwer — Paul
Brown — Alan
Brown — Janine
Brown — Trevor
Browne — Harry Louis Arthur
Bryant — Jeremy John
Burger — Marianne
Burgers — Peter
Butt — Anthony Dan
Calitz — Ralph Frederick
Carstens — Fifty
Carstens — Wilhelm
Carter — Roger
Christie-Smith — James Michael
Cook — William David
Cope — Robert David
Corsten — Peter
Crawford — Lindsay
Cromhout — Peter
Cupido — Hendry
Daly — Alan
Darcy-Evans — Andrew
Davis — Bevan John
Davis — Bruce
Davis — Len
Davis — Michael
Dawe — Brian
de Oliveira — Jose Carlos Novo

de Quintal	Guilherme Joao	Janari	Theo Godfrey	Morillion	Derek	Stacey	Trevor
Deacon	Thomas	Jeftha	Andrew	Morris	Charles	Stanton	Craig Russell
Del Monte	Lance	Johnstone	Victor	Mulholland	Russel James	Sterley	Philip
D'Hooghe	Odon	Jones	Oliver Phyl	Munnik	Lynne	Stride	David Frederick
Donald	Margaret	Jordaan	Goody	Munnik	Michael Barry	Struthers	Neil
Downham	Brian	Joseph	Donavan	Nel	Adriaan Johannes	Swart	Deon
du Plessis	Charl Francois	Joubert	Pieter	Nel	Bart	Theron	Jacques Pierre
du Plessis	Johan	Karpinski	Kris	Nel	Chris Peter	Theron	Peter Charles
du Sart	Kelvin	Katzenellenbogen	Ivan	Nesbitt	Charles Henry	Theron	Rene
du Toit	Jan Hendrik	Kay	Zirk	Nicks	Simon	Theys	Jeremy
du Toit	Vaughan Carl	Keet	Deon	Nixon	Ian	Thomas	Barry David John
Eekers	Anthony	Knol	Francis	North	Michael	Thomas	Patrick
Elliott	Graham John	Kriel	Stephen	Novella	Peter	Tobler	Thomas
Ellis	Deon	Krohn	Roger	Nuns	David	Tresidder	Brian Kenneth
Emery	Peter	Kummer	Andrew	Nuns	Michael Anthony	Trevor-Goode	Bob
Esterhuizen	Johann de Villiers	la Mantia	Nando	Oberholzer	Renier	Trout	Garry
Etsebeth	Dale	Lamminga	Murco	Olbrich	Robert	Unger	Axel
Eyssen	Barry	Lawrance	Ronald Milton	Olsen	Barry	van der Merwe	Jacobus Petrus
Ferguson	Nicolette	le Grange	Jeffrey	Orkin	Darel A	van der Merwe	Penelope Mary
Finch	John	Lemmer	Carinus	Osrin	Richard	van Dongen	Cornelis
Fouchee	Gerda	Lemmer	Robert	Paarman	Jonathan Christopher	van Heerden	Hercules Christiaan
Fourie	Desiree	Lindau	Ian Joel	Palm	Peter	van Niekerk	Coenie
Fradley	Kunnie	Lok	Sharon Ann	Palmer	Mel	van Rooijen	Erik Johan
Fradley	Peter	Lok	Victor John	Parker	Michael Anthony	van Thiel	Willem
Francis	Jerome Daniel	Lorentz	Philip Gordon	Pettit	Michael	van Tonder	Andries
Funke	Norbert	Loubser	Jimmy	Pflocksch	Stefan	van Wyk	Annas He
Garfield	Paul	Loubser	Johann	Potter	Vernon	Vercuiel	Nicolaas J
Garrett	David	Loubser	Russell Mark	Price	Robert Parry	Visagie	Ian
Gates	Andrew	Louw	Adriaan	Ramage	James	von Witt	Robert
Gibb	Scotch	Louw	Margaret	Ranger	David Morris	Weaver	Ashley
Gibbons	Lionel	Lowings	Peter	Read	Jeffery Owen	Weedall	Mark
Giljam	Cherry	Lyttle	Gary Michael	Redfern	David George	Weidenbruck	Eddie Charles
Glanvill	Mark	Mahieu	Harry	Robinson	Brevan Lance	Welgemoed	Moolman
Glasser	David	Mahieu	Sven	Rogers	David Clive	Wiederkehr	Walter
Godfrey	Anthony William	Malan	Gabriel Jakobus	Ross	Robert William	Wohlmann	Alan
Goldschmidt	Chris	Malan	Hermanus Johannes	Rossouw	William	Wright	Kevan Thomas
Gordon	Peter Crichton	Mann	Kenneth Henry	Roux	Shirley Jane		
Govender	Thinasegaran	Mantell	John	Sait	Mogamat Riefaat	**17 TOURS**	
Griffin	Terry	Marks	Robin	Sargeant	Michael		
Griffiths	Robert Clive	Martin	Ian Peter	Scannell	Jan	Abbott	Tony
Hancock	Michael James	Mason	Juan Francois	Schelbert	Iwan	Abrey	John
Hardy	Alan	McCallum	Roy	Scholtz	Randall	Alexander	Robert Edward
Harmse	Werner	McDougall	Graham	Schreuder	Charel	Andrew	Ken
Hendrickse	Chad Elton	McLagan	Neil	Schuurmans	John Henry	Andrews	Stephen
Higgins	John	McQueen	Alister Jaques	Searle	Donald	Annas	Rolf
Hillier	Anthony	Meissner	Peter	Semple	Andrew Lyle	Aspeling	Leslie
Hollis	Gavin	Millenaar	Robyn	Serdyn	Johan de Villiers	Bailey	Jason Peter
Horsfall	John Michael	Mills	Jimmy	Sharpley	Michael Andrews	Bardin	Peter David
Huiskens	Gerhard	Moir	Craig Angus	Simpson	James	Barenblatt	Henry
Ilsley	Jeff	Moore	Archie	Snyman	Joe	Barnard	Maureen Pamela
Jacobs	Paul	Morgan	Stuart	Solomon	Alex Cecil	Bee	Glenn
						Bekker	Sonja

Simpson	Charles	Webb	Grant
Simpson	Edward Barry	Webb	Janice
Smit	Boet	Wiehahn	George J
Southern	Nigel David	Wiehahn	Stephanus George
Staal	Pieter	Wilcox	Kevin Nolan
Stallbom	Kevin	Wilding	Roy
Steyn	Stefan	Wilensky	Marc
Stone	Nicholas Richard	Willard	Tim
Strombeck	Francoisjohannes	Williams	Edrich Miles
Strydom	Willem Nicolas	Williams	Kenneth
Summerton	Brian	Windsor	Wayne
Sylvester	Deon Craig	Worsdale	Anthony
Theron	Adriaan	Yates	Kevin
Tittleton	Shane	Zeh	Adu
Trollope	Peter William	Zwiegers	Jan A S

16 TOURS

Unite	Peter Francis	Abel	Mervyn
Urion	Mcarthur	Abrahams	Emile
Urmson	John	Abrahams	Stephen
van Breda	Lizbe	Anderson	Brett Peter
van den Bosch	Bruce	Anderson	Greg Travers
van der Berg	Gideon Christiaan	Anderson	Stuart
Van der Merwe	Philippus Bauke	Andrew	John
van der Merwe	Sakkie	Andrews	Bruce Meredith
van der Velde	Rob	Andrews	Christopher
van der Walt	Gehri	Angelil	Serge
van der Walt	Johannes	Arnold	Robert
van Ginkel	Graeme	Austin	Evan George
van Lill	Cornelius Jakobus	Avenant	Karin Lynn
van Onselen	Annamarie	Baard	Leon
van Rensburg	Pieter	Bagley	Windsor
van Rheede	Rutger	Baldwin	Ken
van Staden	Frederick	Balt	Renier
van Wieringen	Johanna Maria	Barker	John
van Woudenberg	Paul	Benting	Eben Richard
van Zyl	Albertus Jacobus	Beytell	Andy
van Zyl	Daniel Petrus Jacobus	Biccari	Sandro
Venter	Alex	Biffen	Nigel
Verwey	Brian	Blanckensee	Richard
Viret	Leon	Boshoff	Markus
Volschenk	Ernest Johannes	Botes	Anton
Vorster	Alewyn	Botes	Hannes
Vymetal	Jiri	Botes	Tony
Watkins	Leonard		
Watson	Basil		

Botha	Martinus Johannes Theunis	de Waal	Meyer
Boulle	Andrew	Deetlefs	Tony
Breytenbach	Peter Joshua	Dekker	Arie
Brice	Keith James	Deuchar	Brian William
Brink	Paul	Dokter	Hendrikus
Brook	John	Donn	John Christopher
Bruchhausen	Kurt	dos Santos	Domingos
Buckley	Christopher George	du Plessis	Garry
Burger	Hector Douglas	du Toit	Guillaume
Butler	David	Dunlop	Gavin
Cay	David	Eagar	Rodney
Chaitman	Jeremy Leon	Ehlers	Anton
Chanterie	Leopold	Ehlers	Leon
Cilliers	Stephanus Jose	Eksteen	Roelof
Clark	Suzanne	Ellis	Michael
Clegg	David	Erasmus	Chris
Cloete	Oscar	Erasmus	Pieter Johannes
Cochran	Donald	Evertson	David
Cole	Wesley	Eyden	Linda
Conradie	Rudie	Ferreira	Marius Andre
Cook	Bruce Adrian	Finnegan	Christopher
Cookson	Michael	Fish	Brian John
Costello	Andrew	Fotheringham	Christopher
Cox	Raymond	Fourie	Johan
Coxwell	Christopher Edward	Frans	John
Crawford	Marilyn	Fransen	Hans
Crawford	Martin	Gales	Keith
Crawford	Shirley Kerridwen	Gendron	Claude
Cronk	George Frederick	Glass	Ian Stuart
Dalton	Paul	Glezer-Jones	Neil David
Daniel	Jason	Goodall	Greg
Davies	Alan Phillip	Gordon	Malcolm Nigel Bruce
Day	Roger Ian	Graham	Michael Alexander Vincent
de Beer	Gordon	Grant	David Michael
de Freitas	Anton	Gray	Paul
de Graaf	Neal Brent	Gray	Tony
de Klerk	Willem Johannes	Greenway	Robin
de Kock	Danielle	Gregan	Derek Charles
de Kock	Gabriel	Groenewald	Vincent C
de Kock	Neil Andrew	Groeneweegen	Jon
De la Porte	Andries Jacobus	Hacker	Tim
de Lange	Robert	Halberstadt	Michael Peter
de Lange	Wessel	Haley	Christopher Noel
de Rooy	Robert	Hamilton	Ian
		Hancox	Colin
		Hansen	Theodore Phillip
		Hart	Peter Robert
		Havenga	Jan
		Higgs	Peter
		Hill	Henry
		Hitchcock	Ian Jeanne
		Hodson	Shirley
		Holloway	George
		Holzman	Alan
		Horn	Koos
		Horwitz	Frank
		Houliston	Robert
		Hunt	Robert William
		Huppert	Richard Nicholas
		Immelman	Johan
		Ingpen	Paul Robert Hector
		Jacobs	Farrel Joshua
		Jacobs	Leon
		Janse van Rensburg	Anton
		Jansen	Jacobus Martin
		John	Trevor Alan

Jossel	Ryan	Meyer	Graham	Sass	Michael	van der Bijl	Jan Dirk
Joubert	Werner	Meyer	Pieter	Sayers	Grant	van der Merwe	Petrus Johannes
Jupp	Graham Terry	Middelmann	Paul	Scannell	Jan	van der Sluys	Alex
Katz	Akiva Raphael	Milakovic	Branko	Schnehage	Alfred	van der Wel	Willem G
Keenan	Jo	Miller	Colin	Schroeder	John	van der Westhuizen	David Leon
Kemp	Erill	Millet	Geoff	Schultz	Leon	van Deventer	Sarel
Kemp	Erna	Mills	Derrick Richard Daniel	Seidel	Harald	van Ginkel	Julian Alexander
Kennedy	Ian John	Momsen	Nicholas Johannes	Senneck	Paul	van Hoogstraten	Antony
King	Chris	Morris	Collin	Shaw	Andrew	van Niekerk	Pompies
King	Donald	Mullin	David John	Shaw	Sean	van Rooyen	André
Klein	Max	Munnik	Roy	Silberbauer	Pieter	van Seumeren	Cyril
Kloppers	Johan	Munton	Rob	Simonis	Alexander Walter	van Tonder	Jacobus Petrus
Knight	Gregory	Nel	Jacobus Petrus	Simpson	Richard	van Velden	David Pieter
Knipe	John	Oettle	Theodore J	Smit	Pierre	van Wyk	Jackie
Knoetze	Mike	Oliver	Marian Jean	Smith	Clive L	van Zyl-Smit	Richard Nellis
Koping	Brian	Olivier	Arie	Smith	Ian	Versfeld	Peter Graham
Kuster	Manfred	Oosthuizen	Anton	Smith	Vernon	Viljoen	Ernst
Lambrecht	Karl	Opperman	Chris	Snyman	André	Visagie	Johan Hermias
Lapping	Robin James	Ostini	Giancarlo	Snyman	Henning	Visagie	Willem Johannis
Lawrence	Redvers George	Palm	André	Snyman	Jeanette	Visser	Eric
le Grange	Jacobus Henry	Pearce	Barry Laurence	Sparks	John Winchester	Walton	Ian
Lees	David Ian	Pearson	Mark	Spence	Daniel	Wessels	Tallis
Lemmer	Hendrik	Peebles	Trevor	Stanley	Edwin	Wheeler	John
Lewis	Alan	Perry	Neil	Steele	Peter	White	Hellen
Lewis	Biff	Petersen	Eugene	Steenveld	Lance Robin	Williams	James
Liebentritt	Roland	Petersen	Wayne Edward	Steincke	Willy	Wilsdorf	Robert
Lill	Darren	Pickard	Jan Albertus Jacobus	Stevens	Coral	Wilsnagh	Derek
Lincoln	Bertie	Pienaar	Vosloo	Stevenson	Craig Richard	Winship	George Martin
Lodder	Peter Gideon Emerton	Pollock	Ian M	Steyn	Coenraad Christoffel	Wium	Gert
Louw	David	Pombo	Jaime	Stockli	Robert	Wood	John L
Louw	Nicolaas	Potgieter	Karl	Strauss	Adriaan	Wood	Leslie
Louwrens	Joan	Potgieter	Marthinus	Strauss	Andries Jacobus		
Maartens	Leon	Potts	Patrick	Street	Michael George		
Maccallum	David Ross	Priday	Anthony	Surridge	William Philip Lewis		
Macdonald	Manus	Prins	Christo	Swart	Donald		
Major	Peter Michael	Pritchard	Philip	Swart	Pieter		
Manners-Wood	Rob	Rabe	Jan	Swart	Rupert		
Maritz	John	Rabie	Lodewyk	Sweet	Garth		
Marle	Yvonne	Rademeyer	Carl	Szabo	Elizabeth Catherine		
Martin	James Louis	Ratcliff	Cyril Jerome	Taliotes	Michael		
Marx	Willie	Reeves	Colin	Taljaard	Matthys Johannes		
Mason	James	Reinhardt	David	Taljaard	Piet		
Masterson	Allen Geoffrey	Reynolds	Louis G	Taljaard	Pieter Jurgens		
Matern	Norbert	Robertson	Clive Preston Whyte	Tamsen	Wally		
Matthee	Francois	Robertson	Ian	Thebus	Henry		
Mc Duling	Wayne Arthur	Ross	André Kenneth	Thebus	Ian		
McGregor	Graeme	Ross	Ronnie	Timkoe	Victor George		
McKeown	Stephen	Rossouw	Andrew Peter	Trollope	John Wesley		
Meacham	Ellis Fenwick	Roux	Tielman Johannes	Uliana	Enrico O		
Mearns	Andrew	Royston	Gail Anne	van Breda	Jasper		
Melless	Sally	Sanderson-Smith	Peter	van Coller	Barry		

15 TOURS

Adam	Ian Mcintosh		
Adamo	Raffaele		
Adams	Richard		
Adendorff	Norman		
Ainsbury	Douglas John		
Alexander	Azies		
Alkana	Isaac		
Allen	Keith Erskine		
Anderson	Jock		
Aries	Jerry		
Arnold	John		
Aspeling	Christo Peter		
Austin	Jenny		
Bailey	Bradfield A F		
Baker	Cecil Mccalaghan		
Baker	Glenn		
Baker	Terence		
Ball	James Philip		

Barber	Jenny	Carse	Kenneth	Dickson	Alastair	Hellings	Chris R
Barnard	Gideon Josua	Carstens	Deon	Diederichs	Patrick	Heynike	John Raymond
Barnett	Graham	Chapman	Eric	Diener	André	Heystek	Marthinus
Barth	Detlef	Cheeseman	Richard	Dixon	Brad Sean	Hilton	Rory Conrad
Bartleet	Trevor Clive	Chemelli	Jürgen	Dixon	Mark Neil	Holland	Elton Michael
Bates	Nigel	Chesterton	Elaine	Dobie	Grant	Holst	Victor
Beckett	Jana	Christie	Ian	Dowling	Frank	Holzman	Gavin Adrian
Bee	Michael	Cilliers	Jan	Dreyer	Clive Obrian	Hooper	Les
Bellairs	David Carlyon Collingwood	Clarke	Karin	Drogemoller	Hugo	Howell	Neville Kurt
Beneka	Maxim	Clemen	Quinton	du Bruyn	Doreen	Hugo	Ettienne
Bergh	Vincent	Cloete	Anton	du Pisani	Niel	Hugo	Mark Hilton
Bergoff	Simone Claire	Cloete	Johan Sebastian	du Plessis	Morné	Hutchinson	Douglas William
Bernardo	Walter Alfred Joseph	Cloete	Pieter	du Plooy	Marius	Hynes	Stuart
Beytell	Mia	Coetzee	Cobie	du Toit	Dawie	Immelman	Martin
Bezuidenhout	André	Coetzee	John	du Toit	Dirk Lourens	Isaacs	Nigel
Bigara	Bernard	Coetzee	Ubert	du Toit	Leon	Jackson	Denys
Binedell	Johan	Collyer	Rodney	du Toit	Miriam	Jacobs	Gretha
Blom	Jay	Conrad	Julian Edward	Duddy	Les	Jamieson	Anthony
Boonzaaier	Petrus	Conradie	Alan	Dun	Colin	Jansen van Vuuren	Johannes Petrus
Bosch	Emma	Conradie	Jacobus	Duncan	Andrew	Jeenes	Coleen
Botha	Andries Jacobus	Cormack	Michael John	Durler	Werner	Jeftha	Jonathan
Botha	Jan	Cost	Marco Stephan	Easton	Gerrit Floris	Johnson	Garth
Botha	Johan Francois	Couldridge	David	Eder	Bernd Joachim	Jones	Evan
Bothwell	Richard	Cowper	JG	Egli	Hans	Joss	Dale Michael
Bowers	Reginald	Crawford	Walter James	Ehlers	Anton	Joul	Wilby
Boyce	Donald Arderne	Cronje	Roche	Emery	Martin Peter	Jowell	Jeremy
Bresick	Graham	Cronk	Darren	Engelbrecht	Liezel	Kapp	Wynand Johannes
Broad	Michael	Cullis	Sydney Neville Raynor	Eras	Boudewyn	Kerr	Bill
Brown	Christopher	Cummings	George	Erasmus	Noel Benjamin	Kingwill	Ronnie
Brown	Douglas	Dalton	David	Erda	Edward	Kinsey	Edward
Brown	Ian Martin	Dalton	Sean Edward	Ernst	Achim	Kirk-Cohen	Steve
Brown	Michael L	Daniel	Kevin	Everingham	John	Koch	Aneen
Brown	Richard Denis	Daniels	Joseph	Fataar	Shamiel	Koch	Frank
Buley	Paul	Davies	Peter Derek William	Ferreira	Oscar	Koorts	Gerhardus Jeremiah
Burger	Andries Schalk	Dax	Henrietta	Fortune	Kevin Christian	Kotze	Stirling Athol
Burger	Francois	de Agrela	Ricardo	Fortune	Lindsay Neville	Krauss	Brenner
Burger	Hester Maria	de Beer	Gordon	Fourie	Johannes Marthinus	Krige	Paul
Burger	Jacobus Adriaan	de Villiers	Bernard Matthys	Fourie	Matthys Johannes	Kruse	Gavin F
Burgher	Cecil Carl	de Villiers	Jacques	Fox	Leonora	Kussendrager	Jack
Burman	Errol Wesley	de Waal	Margaret Patricia	Fradley	Taryn	Kuys	Frederick
Bushney	Leon	Deist	Leon	Frick	Belinda	Lambert	Peter
Caine	Janet	Dell	Gary	Gaillard	Johan	Lambrecht	Louis
Calothi	Nick	Denton	James	Gamsu	Brian	Lamprecht	Marthinus C
Campbell	Carol	Dercksen	Daff	Gardner	John Stuart	Langdon	Keith Andrew
Carden	Kenneth	Deysel	Gregory	Garrod	Kevin Peter	Langman	Angela
				Garzancich	Derick	Laverty	Patrick
				Gaskell	Barry	Lawrence	Elred
				Gaven	Clive	Lawrence	Paull
				Geater	Cyndy	Lazarus	John H
				Geldenhuys	Karin Marcelle	le Roux	Martin
				George	David	Lederle	Douglas Eason
				George	Nathaniel Graydon	Leff	Christopher
				Gerber	Nicky	Lennard	Chris
				Gibb	Robert	Levings	Kenneth John
				Giddey	Richard	Levitan	Rael
				Gold	Charl	Levy	Anthony
				Goldstuck	Oscar	Lloyd-Roberts	Rosemary
				Goosen	Michiel Daniel	Lockley	Dick
				Gould	William Ronald	Lodwick	Colin
				Grant	Sandy	Lomberg	Ian Gerald Smuts
				Groener	Florence	Lotter	Robert Clive
				Harding	Willem Nicolaas	Lotter	Vernon Eric
				Hardy	Clive David	Loubser	Max
				Harvey	Ric	Louw	Bradley
				Havenaar	Theo	Lutskes	Alexander
				Havenga	Jan	Luus	Victor

Maddock	Graham	Oosthuizen	Karel	Scheiner	Brian	van der Westhuizen	Georg Ernst Alexander
Magni	Stefano	Oosthuizen	Maurice Leon	Schmidt	Ryan Earle	van Dyk	Flippie
Maguire	Christine	Oosthuizen	Susara Johanna	Schneider	Carl	van Loggerenberg	Ronald
Malan	Danie F	O'Sullivan	Edward	Scholtz	Jaco	van Niekerk	Bernhard M P
Malherbe	Philip	Oxenham	Charles	Schwenke	Jaco	van Niekerk	Joel
Mallows	Frank Arthur	Parker	Paul Spencer	Scott	Susan	van Niekerk	Willem
Mamacos	George	Pearce	Cameron	See	Bruce Edward	van Onselen	Leonardo
Manson-Kullin	Lynne Moira	Pegel	Theo	Shainfeld	Cecil	van Reenen	Ross
Manus	Fred	Perold	Joubert	Shaw	Ian Thomas	van Riel	Allan
Marchant	Reagan David	Petersen	Michael Glen	Shedden	Edward	van Schoor	Chris
Mare	Lisa Antoinette	Phillips	Charles Anthony	Shillington	Frank	van Velden	Hannes
Marsh	Nigel	Pinto	Jose Saul	Shira	Aboebaker	van Wyk	Steven
Maske	Richard	Plimsoll	John	Slabber	Schalk	van Zijl	Paul
Maxwell	Garth	Pohl	Carl Triegaardt	Slabber	Willem Frederick	van Zuylen	Harry
Mazewski	Andrew Richard	Pompa	Marcello	Smal	Jan	van Zyl	Boet
Mc Dowall	Andrew	Poolman	Erwin	Smit	George H	van Zyl	Gideon
Mc Queen	Kevin	Poulter	Kevin	Smith	Anthony Mark	van Zyl	Jeromy
McCarthy	Gregory	Pretorius	Gys	Snailum	Alan	van Zyl	Johannes Petrus
McCarthy	Johan	Preyer	Neil	Snyman	Johan	van Zyl	Marius
McClarty	Raymond	Price	Aubrey	Solomons	Ronald	Veller	Bernhard
McKenzie	Kenneth R	Price	Ray	Spaan	Stephan Bernard	Venter	Jacobus Johannes
McKinney	David	Priday	Justin	Stansfield	Gavin John	Viljoen	George
Meiring	Alex	Pringle	Mark	Staphorst	Mike	Vincent	Robert
Melvill	Robert G	Probert	Robert James	Steenkamp	Noel William	Visser	David A
Merrifield	Anne	Rabie	Chris	Stevens	Jack	Vockins	Halmar
Miceli	Bruno	Raimondo	Michael	Stewart	Graeme	Vosloo	Carel Petrus
Michie	Ian	Rainier-Pope	Paul	Stichini	João Carlos	Vroom	Tony
Miller	Lawrence	Ratcliffe	Norma	Stricker	Kenneth	Wale	Eric
Minnaar	Martin	Raubenheimer	Willem	Strydom	Casper Andries	Walsh	Neil
Mitchell	David Gordon	Rauff	Howard	Strydom	Eduan	Ward	Graham John
Morawski	Ted	Reid	Charles	Swan	Patrick Graves	Warnich	Petrus Serdyn
Morgan	William Tyler	Reid	Clifford	Swarts	Neil	Wentzel	Petrus Johannes
Morillion	Lesley	Reyneke	Bruce	Symington	Stanley John	Wexler	Brian
Morison	David	Richter	Antoinette	Tack	Philippe	White	John
Morris	Mark Richard	Ripsold	Patrick	Taylor	William	White	Nicholas
Moss	Stephen J	Rix	Wayne	Tennent	Jonathan G C	Whittaker	Julia R B
Muller	Brett	Robertson	Donovan	Terblanche	William Henry	Wiederkehr	Marc
Mullins	Lionel	Robertson	Julian	Thompson	John	Williamson	Peter
Murray	Peter David	Robinson	Leslie	Timmie	Allistair	Wilson	Carol
Murray	Spencer	Rood	Colin Karl	Tjasink	Brian	Winkel	Fred
Nel	Duane Richter	Rosenstein	Shaun	Toet	Kees	Winter	Fred
Nel	Paul	Ross	Brandon Daryl	Unsworth	Duncan	Wolf	Christian
Nepgen	Karl Emil	Rossouw	Glynn Arnaud Roger	Valentine	Clive	Wolmarans	Annerie
Newcombe	Charlie	Rothenburg	Brad	van Cuyck	Etienne	Wooding	Mario Juan
Nicolle	Peter	Roux	Paul	van de Merwe	Theo	Wooldridge	William
Noah	Paula	Rowley	Lionel	van der Bijl	Douwtje	Worrall	Terrence
Norris	Christopher R	Rubidge	John Hamilton	van der Helm	Andrew	Wright	Peter John
Norval	Tarquin	Runkel	Matthew	van der Merwe	Jan Schellink	Wykerd	Malan
O'Connor	Scott	Rushin	Patrick Louis	van der Mescht	Marius	Yon	Barry Timothy
Oettle	Peter	Saayman	Frederik Thomas	van der Spuy	Hendrik Kruger	Young	Robert
Olivier	Ceddric Ian	Santiago	Jorge	van der Walt	Gerda	Zeelie	Peter John
Oosthuizen	Elemans van Rooyen	Saunders	Neville	van der Westhuizen	Christopher	Ziervogel	Carel

GENERAL ACKNOWLEDGEMENTS

The Big Ride by former *Argus* editor Andrew Drysdale (published by Don Nelson in 1998 to mark the 21st Cycle Tour) provided a valuable source of background information as did the archives of *the Cape Argus* newspaper (in particular Zara Nicholson's interviews with the Magnificent Seven) and the official Cycle Tour magazines.

I am grateful to all the staff at the SA National Library for their assistance in accessing old newspapers.

Cape Argus Editor Chris Whitfield and his deputy Dave Chambers both enthusiastically backed the project. Independent Newspapers, Cape photo editors Jim McLagan and Ian Landsberg were also extremely helpful. Debbie McLean of Trace Images and Soraya Moses at Independent assisted with the photo research.

My thanks to all the dedicated Cycle Tour staff including Dave Bellairs, Ken Sturgeon, Chad Scalzini, Adri Bootsma and, especially, Pat White.

Brett Hilton-Barber planted the seed of the idea for this book and helped get it going.

Colleen Hendriksz, Sandy Shepherd & Sarah O'Neill of Juta Double Storey guided the publishing process and Jennifer Stern did the text editing. Pete Bosman, who has ridden the Tour himself, was an outstanding designer to work with.

Cycle Tour staff and Johnny Koen assisted with checking for errors but if there are any remaining the responsibility is entirely mine.

And, most importantly, my wonderful family (Helen, Kate, Ty & Lucy) supported me through the training and completion of seven Cycle Tours (my son at the age of four, having waited patiently for an hour and seen thousands of bikes go past up Wynberg Hill, asked me so optimistically when I finally arrived 'are you winning dad?'). They also encouraged me through the research, writing and production of this book.

MIKE WILLS
NOVEMBER 2007
mikewills@iafrica.com

PHOTO ACKNOWLEDGEMENTS

Copyright © in photography/print media as listed below:

Nato Barnard/IMAGES24.co.za: 90 (top middle), 92 (below). **Shawn Benjamin:** front cover, 2-3, 8-9, 12, 15, 16, 17, 19, 20–21, 22, 23, 26, 28 (top), 31 (bottom), 32, 35, 36, 37, 38, 39, 41, 42, 44, 45, 47, 48, 50, 51, 52–53, 54, 59, 60, 61, 62, 63, 65, 66, 68, 70, 71, 76, 106, 109 (top right & bottom left), 111, 114, 118 (top left), 120 (bottom), 121, 122, 123 (top and bottom right), 124 (bottom), 125, 135 (right), 140, 141 (top left & right), 143. **Bill Mylrea:** 81 (middle). **John Stegmann:** 81 (top). **University of Cape Town:** 87 (top right).

All other photographs courtesy of **Independent Newspapers, Cape** whose staff photographers have covered the race over the past 30 years. Regrettably it isn't possible to determine the names of every photographer whose work appears but they include Mathilde Dusol, Thembinkosi Dwayisa, Brenton Geach, Oliver Hermanus, Andrew Ingram, Angelo Kalmeyer, Henk Kruger, Ian Landsberg, Leon Lestrade, Jim McLagan, Leon Muller, Doug Pithey, Sophia Stander, Peter Stanford, Alan Taylor, Hannes Thiart, Cindy Waxa, Roy Wigley, Gary van Wyk and Obed Zilwa. My apologies to anyone I have inadvertently omitted.